FRAME BY FRAME
AN INTRODUCTION TO FILM

JASON GONZALEZ

—INVER HILLS COMMUNITY COLLEGE—

Kendall Hunt
publishing company

Cover image © 2013. Used under license from Shutterstock, Inc.

Kendall Hunt
publishing company

www.kendallhunt.com
Send all inquiries to:
4050 Westmark Drive
Dubuque, IA 52004-1840

Copyright © 2013 by Jason Gonzalez

ISBN 978-1-4652-7774-9

Kendall Hunt Publishing Company has the exclusive rights to reproduce this work, to prepare derivative works from this work, to publicly distribute this work, to publicly perform this work and to publicly display this work.

All rights reserved. No part of this publication may be reproduced, stored in a retrieval system, or transmitted, in any form or by any means, electronic, mechanical, photocopying, recording, or otherwise, without the prior written permission of the copyright owner.

Printed in the United States of America
10 9 8 7 6 5 4 3 2 1

CONTENTS

Chapter 1   A Brief History of Film   1

Chapter 2   Film Language and Criticism   11

Chapter 3   Mise-en-Scene   21

Chapter 4   Editing   31

Chapter 5   Motion in Pictures   39

Chapter 6   Collaboration: Direction and Design   47

Chapter 7   Screenplay   55

Chapter 8   Narrative   65

Chapter 9   Acting   71

Chapter 10   Lighting & Sound   79

Chapter 11   The Digital Age   87

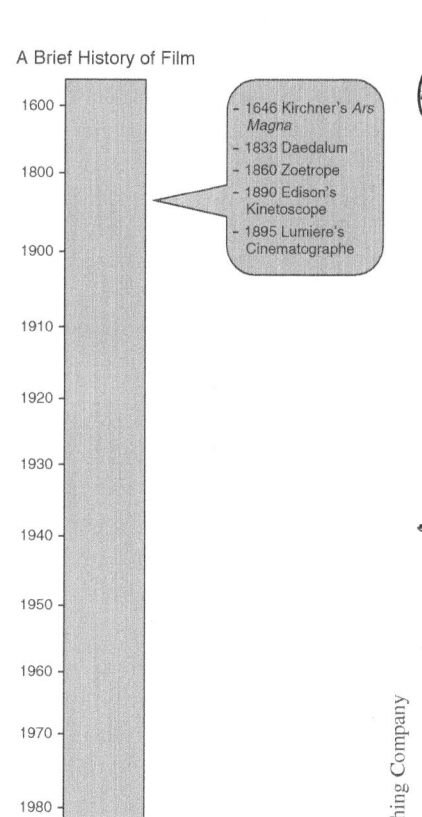

A BRIEF HISTORY OF FILM

CHAPTER 1

A Brief History of Film

1600
- 1646 Kirchner's *Ars Magna*
- 1833 Daedalum
1800
- 1860 Zoetrope
- 1890 Edison's Kinetoscope
1900
- 1895 Lumiere's Cinematographe
1910
1920
1930
1940
1950
1960
1970
1980
1990
2000
Present

Even though the medium of film has been around less than 150 years, it has a rich and extensive history. Many film programs devote two to four semesters to the study of film history—interesting and helpful in understanding film medium. For the purposes of this text, we will touch on only a few highlights in the history of film—In every sense of the word, a brief history of film.

MOVING PICTURES

In 1646 Athanasius Kircher authored a book entitled, *Ars Magna Lucis et Umbrae*. This text focused on the technology of projecting images onto a wall or screen. In it, he discussed the machinery used at the time, the so-called Magic Lantern, and how it could be improved upon. He also explored the idea of using the device for entertainment purposes. At the time, these devices were often used to convince viewers that they were seeing apparitions or sorcery. Kircher debunked these ideas by showing how the device worked, thus removing the "magical" properties that it seemed to possess.

The fascination with moving images can be traced back to the late second century when the Chinese invented the Zoetrope. This device had a rotating fan blade mounted over a lamp. Attached to the blades was a sort of lampshade with images cut out. The heat from the lamp would turn the blades and the shade, causing shadows and images to be cast about the room on walls or screens. In modern times, you can find this sort of lamp in many children's stores for infants to watch as they fall asleep in their cribs. The modern Zoetrope was created by William Homer in 1833 and was originally called a "daedalum." This mechanism had a circular hollow drum with slits cut in it. A strip of images was inserted into the drum and then spun. The viewer would look through the slits and see the image "moving." The daedalum was improved upon and renamed a Zoetrope—meaning wheel of life—in the 1860s.

The technology continued to improve from Magic Lantern to Zoetrope to Phenakistoscope to Praxinoscope to the earliest cameras such as Thomas Edison's Kinetoscope, but film as we know it started to really take off in 1895 with Louis Lumiere's Cinematographe. It gives us actual film recording and a flexibility that Edison's 110-pound camera did not. Lumiere began to film happenings in everyday life. *Workers Leaving the Lumiere Factory* and *Arrival of a Train* are two of the better known "films."

At the time, these moving pictures even of such mundane events, were considered wonders beyond belief. Most people around the world had never seen anything like it, and they were astounded and even frightened by it. There is a story of people running and screaming from a tent when a film of a locomotive coming toward the camera was shown. These early films were so popular in France that the companies that made the films began to send agents all over the world to show the films to an eager and ever-widening audience.

The original performances were held in tents, basements—essentially any place with an open wall or a place to set up a screen. Not until 1914 when the first movie palace, the Mark Strand Theater, was opened to the public, did films have a place of their own to be displayed. The Strand, as it was later called, cost more than $1 million to build, seated 3,000 patrons, and included an orchestra pit, second-floor balcony seating, and two large lobbies where guests could mingle before the show. It was such a success that in two short years the number of movie palaces in the United States had grown to top 21,000.

THE SOUND OF CHANGE

The next big advancements in film were the introductions of color film and sound. In 1927, *The Jazz Singer* became the first "talkie." It was not the first feature film to have sound, though, as once the technology was available, several studios took older films, added music and sound effects to them, and re-released them. These films drew a large box office, but the amount of money it took to add the sound in post-production ate up any profits. *The Jazz Singer* was shot with the sound recorded synchronously, allowing for not only music and sound effects but, for the first time, spoken dialogue. It would completely alter the way in which movies were made and received. The recent feature films *Hugo* and *The Artist* give an idea of the world of silent films and how sound changed the film industry.

As the film industry grew and continued to develop, it became apparent that it had to be better organized and keep records of what was being done. In 1927, the Academy of

A Brief History of Film

- 1914 The first movie palace built.
- 1927 The Jazz Singer becomes the first "talkie."
- 1929 The first Academy Awards.

Motion Picture Arts and Sciences was created. The Academy realized that it needed something to announce to the world that film was not just a hobby or a fad that would soon disappear. To do so, the Academy began recognizing the artists and artisans who worked in the industry for their outstanding achievements.

The first Academy Awards ceremony was held on May 16, 1929. The event was much more low-key than today's gala. The black-tie dinner was more a coronation than an awards show because the winners were actually announced three months earlier, eliminating any suspense. In fact, the first person to win an Academy Award, actor Emil Jannings, did not even attend the event and received his award several weeks earlier before heading back home to Germany for a vacation. Over the years the Oscars, as they have come to be called, have grown to become a four-to-five hour, multi-million-dollar event watched by more than 40 million people worldwide.

THE RISE AND FALL OF THE STUDIO SYSTEM

At around the same time in Hollywood, five major motion picture companies had established themselves as the power base of the industry. This group of conglomerates began what has been called the "studio system" and the "Golden Age of Hollywood." From 1928–1948 these studios put out more than 50 films a year. They not only produced the films but also controlled the distribution of the films. They could control which company's films were shown in which theaters. This nearly absolute power gave the studios a level of control unmatched before or since. Actors in the "studio system" were signed to seven-year contracts.

These contracts meant that the actors could work only for the studio they signed with (unless that studio "rented" them out to another studio) but essentially meant that the actors had to be in whatever films the studio wanted to put them in regardless of whether the actor wanted to do it or not. Since these studios all had the same kind of contracts and they controlled almost all of the films being produced, actors had little choice but to accept what they were offered. The studios could, and did, often put provisions in the contracts that would include what the actors could do in their private lives.

Despite the many drawbacks, there were also benefits to being a part of the studio system. While the rest of the world suffered through the Great Depression, Hollywood did not. If anything, the movie industry grew in power, prestige, and money from 1929 to 1939. A seven-year contract, for all that was bad in it, provided a steady job for seven years. Top actors were paid hundreds of thousands of dollars a year, which in today's economy would top $5 million.

The studio system hit its peak in the late 1930s and 1940s. *Gone with the Wind* opened in 1939 and remains the most-watched film of all time. By the mid-1940s, nearly 90 million people a week were going to movies while

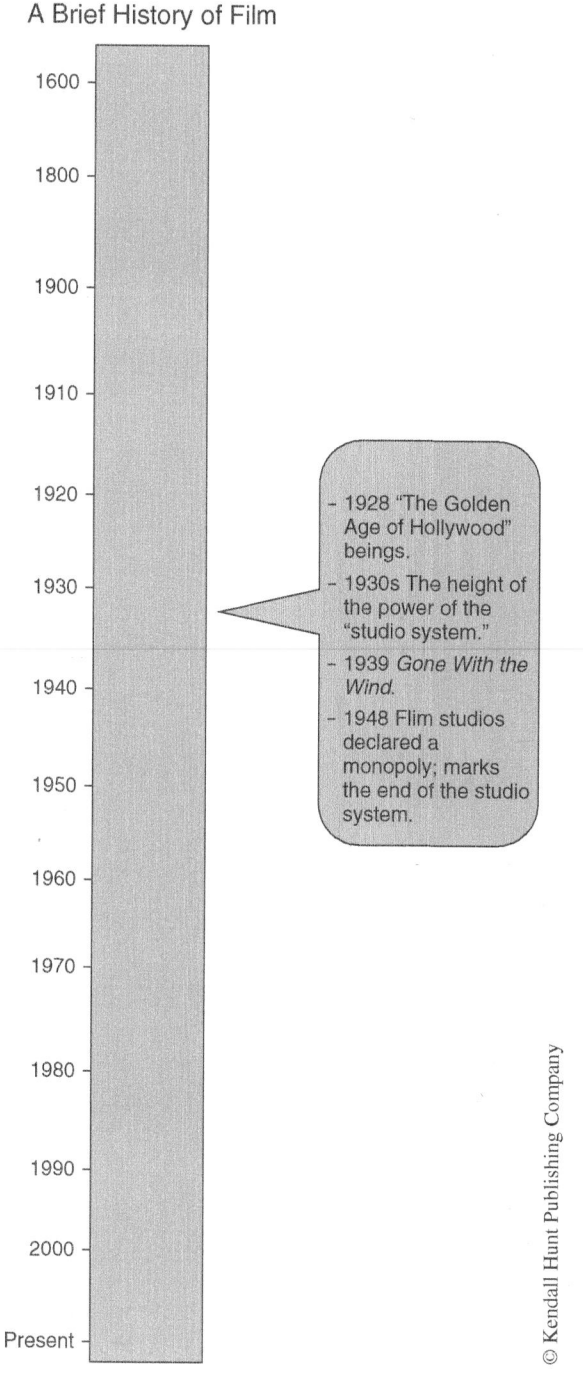

A Brief History of Film

- 1928 "The Golden Age of Hollywood" beings.
- 1930s The height of the power of the "studio system."
- 1939 *Gone With the Wind.*
- 1948 Flim studios declared a monopoly; marks the end of the studio system.

4   Chapter 1

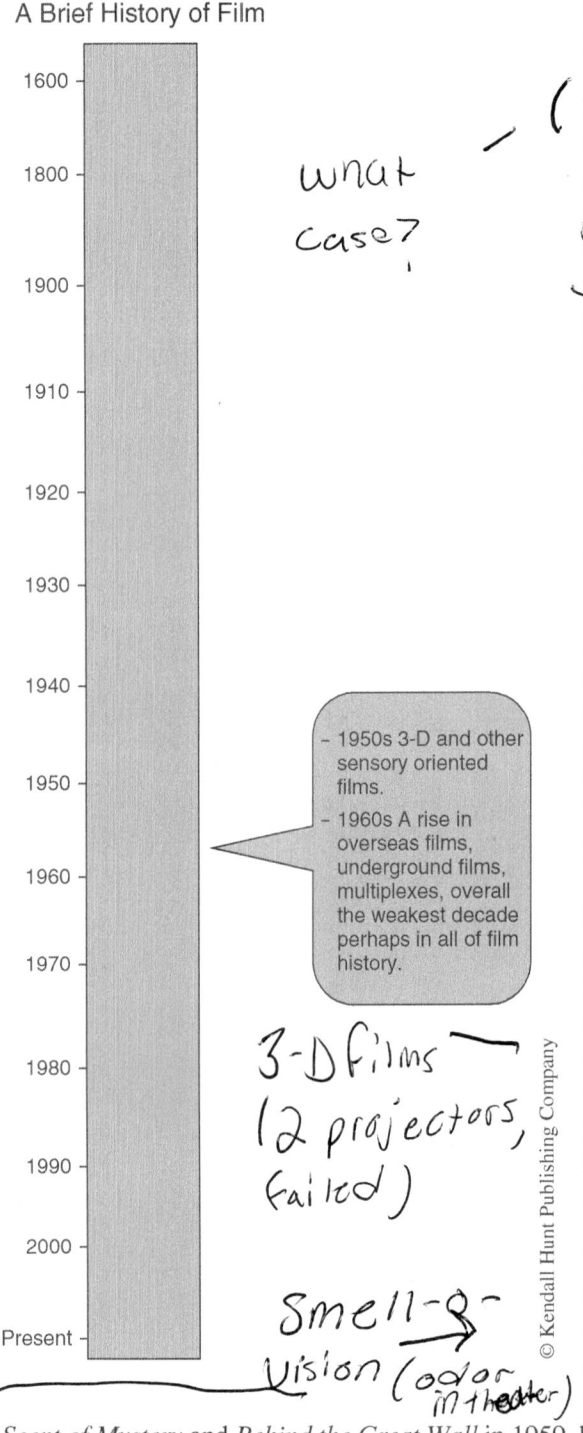

A Brief History of Film

there were barely 5,000 television sets in the entire country. However, in 1948 it would all change almost overnight.

In 1948 the film studios were declared a monopoly by the U.S. Supreme Court. They were ordered to sell their theaters and were no longer allowed to control the distribution of their films in the same way. Now movie theaters could show whatever movies they wanted to show. In one year the income of the five major studios dropped by nearly 70%. The number of films being produced by the "big five" dropped by 75% in three years, and one of the five, RKO Pictures, was completely dissolved. Although the studios survived and continue to exist to this day, their power and influence has never approached what it was in the 1930s and 1940s.

THE NEXT BIG THING

As the studios lost some of their power, television became more and more prevalent throughout the country and the world. Now more people were able to get their entertainment in the comfort of their own home. The film industry had to do something to get people out of their homes and back into the theaters. One of their first attempts was the advent of 3-D movies. While it can be argued that the "first" 3-D films were actually shown all the way back to 1915, it wasn't until the early 1950s that the concept really took off. The films were very well received and very successful. However, the run of 3-D films was short-lived because of the technology. It required two projectors showing the same film at exactly the same time. Any mistake in synchronization, any repair the film might have to go through, would ruin the effect. It proved too difficult to continue on a large scale until the technology came along to allow a film to be shown on just one projector.

In an effort to find the "next big thing" to pull audiences into theaters, companies moved from the eyes to the nose. Smell-o-vision, Smellarama, Odorama and Aromarama—to name only a few, were attempts at releasing smells into the theater triggered by the soundtrack of the film. The first attempts, *Scent of Mystery* and *Behind the Great Wall* in 1959, had varying levels of success. The technical difficulties were obvious: Some areas of the theater wouldn't get the smell until too late, other areas wouldn't get enough to actually smell anything, the vents made loud hissing noises, and other difficulties. These films themselves were of little help, as both were panned almost across the board and the "scent-based films" never made an impact.

THE 1960S

By the time the 1960s rolled around, the film industry, like the United States itself, was in turmoil. The studio system was by all accounts dead, television had a stranglehold on the American public, and it seemed that films might fade into an afterthought. In the early 1960s, U.S.-released films were at an all-time low and, increasingly, the focus seemed to be moving to "made-for-television" movies.

The industry was trying to hold on with big-budget historical films like *Spartacus* in 1960. The next big hope was the epic production of *Cleopatra*. Unfortunately for Hollywood, the explosive relationships among cast members, the technical difficulties, and over-spending on virtually everything caused the budget to balloon up past $44 million. It was the most expensive film ever made at the time and, when figuring for inflation, would still be among the most expensive films ever. It was too long, at well over 3 hours, and it failed miserably. *Cleopatra* signaled the end of the epic historical drama for quite some time.

The large increase in the cost of making movies in Hollywood moved the studios to take their films overseas, specifically to England, where it was much less expensive to make a film. The result of this move was to signal a boom in foreign and foreign language films in the 1960s. This shift away from Hollywood would result in smaller films with smaller budgets. Smaller budgets would then lead to more experimentation in film and in the subject matter of the films. During this decade we see an increase in "underground" films—that is, films that are darker, grittier, and deal with subjects that Hollywood had ignored.

The 1960s also saw a large portion of the population moving from the city to the suburbs. This shift caused a change in the theaters themselves. The once-great movie palaces began to die out, and the multiplex, which better fit the new suburbia, grew rapidly. The hope was that this improvement in location and increase in options would bring more people out of their homes and away from their television sets.

By this time, film as a medium was reaching an age where its earliest leaders, creators, and innovators were leaving the business or passing away. The likes of John Ford, Orson Wells, Howard Hawks, King Vidor, and even Alfred Hitchcock were being replaced by a new wave of directors and a new vision of film. Around the world, Frederico Fellini, Akira Kurosawa, Ingmar Bergman, and Stanley Kubrick were making waves with new stories and new ways of making films. In the United States, Woody Allen, Sidney Lumet, and soon Martin Scorsese, Steven Spielberg, and Francis Ford Coppola were beginning to take over the reins and move the industry in a new and exciting direction.

The 1960s would give us the epics of the early years, the silliness of the beach movies, musicals such as *West Side Story* and *The Sound of Music*, "spaghetti" westerns, the counter-culture films such as *Easy Rider*, a new ratings system for movies, and more. Despite those offerings, it would be widely viewed as one of the weakest decades in terms of artistic advancement and financial success.

THE 1970S

The 1970s would turn the tide with new voices in cinema and birth of the blockbuster event movie. The top-grossing film of 1966 made $6.5 million; the top grossing film of 1975 made $260 million domestically and nearly half a billion worldwide. From the artistic side of the industry, this decade saw an explosion of films that reflected the point-of-view of the

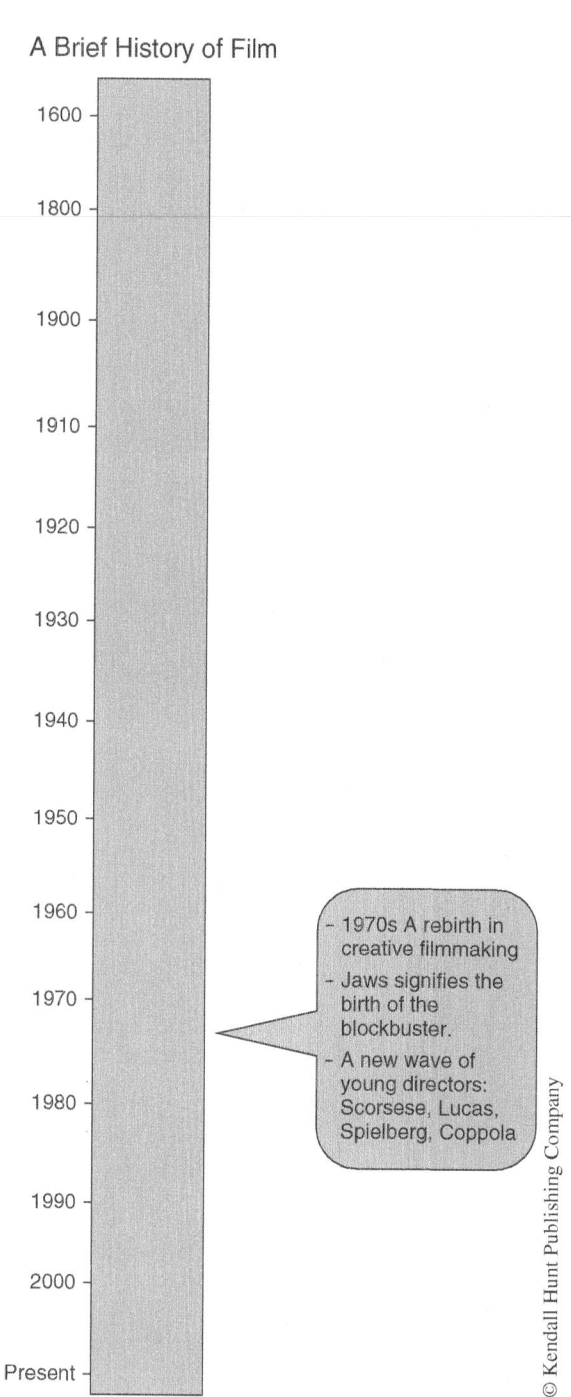

A Brief History of Film

- 1970s A rebirth in creative filmmaking
- Jaws signifies the birth of the blockbuster.
- A new wave of young directors: Scorsese, Lucas, Spielberg, Coppola

young filmmakers and young audiences. The men who made these films—Scorsese, Cimino, Spielberg, Lucas, Coppola, DePalma, and many, many more—were all under the age of 30 when the decade began. This period was particularly volatile in the United States, with the Vietnam War, Watergate, and the hostages in Iran—to name just a few—and cinema reflecting this turmoil and darkness in films such as *All the President's Men*, *The Deer Hunter,* and *Taxi Driver.*

Even the comedies in this time had more of an edge and a message. The films of Woody Allen were on an entirely different level than what we had seen just a few years earlier with *Gidget* and *Beach Blanket Bingo*. Mel Brooks virtually cornered the market on parodies of films from the previous decades such as *Young Frankenstein* and *Blazing Saddles*. His *High Anxiety* mocks virtually every film that Alfred Hitchcock ever made. England brought us the absurdist comedies of Monty Python, which were ridiculous, sublime, and often quite controversial.

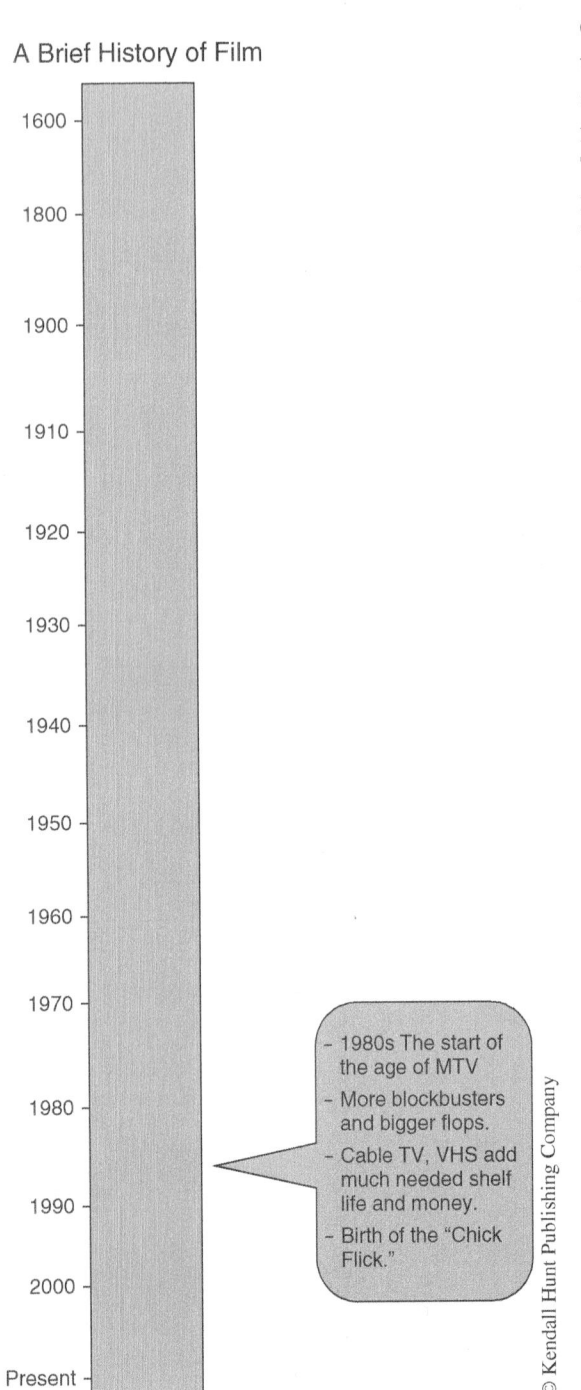

A Brief History of Film

1600
1800
1900
1910
1920
1930
1940
1950
1960
1970
1980
1990
2000
Present

- 1980s The start of the age of MTV
- More blockbusters and bigger flops.
- Cable TV, VHS add much needed shelf life and money.
- Birth of the "Chick Flick."

On the financial end, the blockbuster event movie pulled the industry out of the doldrums in which it had been stuck since the late 1940s. *Jaws* became the highest grossing film of all time by being the first film to top $200 million. Two years later, *Star Wars* eclipsed it, becoming the first film to top $300 million and eventually $400 million. The other big financial revolutions that would eventually translate into a boon for smaller, creative, independent films as well were the introductions of cable television and the VCR. Prior to those advances, a film's lifespan was relatively short. It would be made, distributed, shown a few weeks, and then, if it was lucky, it would show up again years later in a sort of retrospective. *Gone With the Wind* took nearly 40 years to go from the big screen to television. Cable television and the VCR allowed films to greatly extend their lives and greatly increase their earning potential. Increased earning potential meant increased budgets; they more than doubled in a span of just two years.

The 1970s introduced a much-needed infusion of new blood in terms of actors, writers, directors, and markets; it took a floundering industry and set it on a path of unparalleled growth. If you look at a list of the all-time highest grossing films, you will find that none of the top 125 were made before 1972, and the top grossing film of the 1960s, *The Sound of Music*, does not approach the top 200.

THE 1980S

The blockbuster trend continued into the 1980s with films such as *Raiders of the Lost Ark*, *E.T.–The Extra-terrestrial*, *The Empire Strikes Back,* and more. The rapid improvement in special effects (CGI) became a major part of most blockbusters, but the creativity and artistic expression of the 1970s faded quickly into the background as the chase for the next big hit began in earnest. The introduction of MTV split the moneymaking end of the business in two ways. Either a large amount of money was spent on big special effects and big stars with the hope of creating the next *Jaws* or *Star Wars* or the industry went for cheap, flashy, formulaic films, like *Flashdance, Fame, Footloose* or *Purple Rain,* that appealed to new, even younger MTV audiences, The problem, it soon became clear, was that simply throwing money at a film was not enough to make it a blockbuster. The decade saw some of the biggest financial disasters that the industry had ever encountered. *Heaven's Gate, Ishtar,* and *The Adventures of Baron Munchhausen* each lost close to $40 million. The losses were offset, at least somewhat, by the increasing growth of cable television and home video. In just a few years the highest selling VHS went from under a million copies to over 15 million copies. Audiences continued to grow as technology improved, and multiplexes grew at an almost exponential rate.

The MTV generation continued to show its power with the success of teen sex comedies like *Fast Times at Ridgemont High* and teen-oriented comedies like *Sixteen Candles* and *The Breakfast Club.* And the horror film franchises never end. *Halloween, Friday the 13th* and *Nightmare on Elm Street* combined for more than 25 films between them.

The other new demographic to flex its muscles in the 1980s consisted of women. While women had always been a large part of the film-going public, most films were still aimed at their male counterparts. This changed with the advent of the so-called "Chick Flick" films aimed directly at female audiences, appealing to their more emotional side. Films like *Terms of Endearment* and *Beaches* were successful enough to warrant making more films like them. No longer did female audiences have to settle for romantic comedies. They now had full-blown emotional tearjerkers that could be just as financially viable as the teen movies and blockbusters.

THE AGE OF "MORE IS BETTER"

If the 1980s started the big money boom in Hollywood, the 1990s took it to another level. The average film budget that was less than $2 million in the 1970s had grown to nearly $20 million in the 1980s, and in the next decade it topped $50 million dollars with many films topping the $100-million-dollar budget mark. There are two primary reasons for the rapid spike in costs: special effects and mega-stars. Tom Hanks, Jack Nicholson, Julia Roberts, and others saw their own salaries top what it used to cost to make an entire film. For a large part of the decade, in order to make a major motion picture, it had to have a big name, high-priced star attached to it.

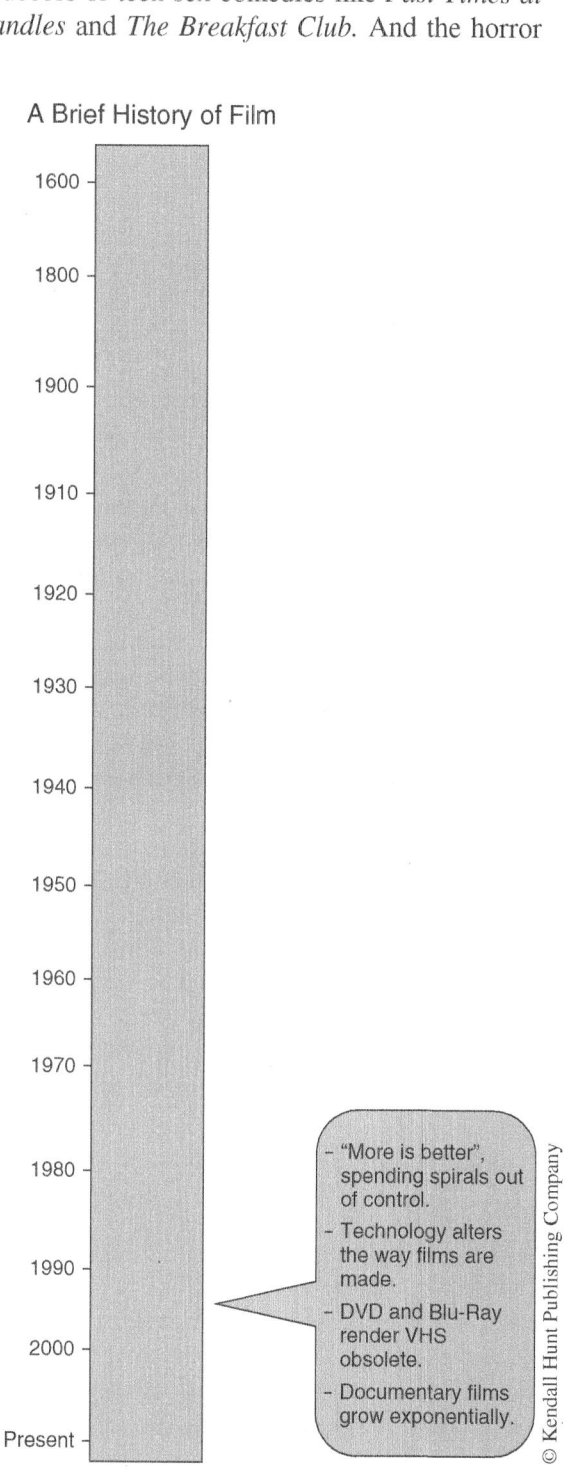

The significance of this time in filmmaking primarily comes down to these two elements: technology and money. Money, as you have clearly realized by now, has been a driving force ever since sound was added to film. What made the 1990s different is how the money was made and how much of it was made. It was now possible for a film to make $100 million in less than a week. In 1989, no film had topped $800 million. By the end of the decade, a film had topped the $2 billion mark. While the biggest successes—*Titanic*, *Jurassic Park*, *Star Wars–Episode I*—had special effects, : two of the most successful films of the decade had almost no special effects at all. *The Sixth Sense* was a story-driven thriller with a twist ending that earned 17 times what it had cost to make. *The Blair Witch Project* was a "found-footage" horror film that was driven by an Internet-based marketing campaign to bring in more than 4,000 times what it had cost. That kind of return on investment will gain anyone's attention. The result was that anyone not trying to make the next *Titanic* was trying to make the next *Sixth Sense* or *Blair Witch Project*. The results were mixed, to say the least.

The technological advances of the decade were monumental. In ten short years we went from the first film to have a digital soundtrack to the first entirely digitally edited film to win an Academy Award to a film that had entirely digitally created characters. We also had movies made on hand-held digital video cameras, giving a more "real," if considerably flatter, look to the action. The first time audiences saw actors running seamlessly alongside a herd of dinosaurs, they were completely blown away. Five years later those effects looked ordinary and uninteresting.

As the new millennium began, the speed of technological advances in film continued to increase. The beginning of the decade saw the first full-length major release shot entirely on a high-definition digital camera at 24 frames per second. The middle of the decade saw the last film to be released on VHS, as DVD and Blu-Ray became the formats of choice. The end of the decade saw the revolution in 3-D filming with *Avatar*, the film that would go on to be the top-grossing movie of all time.

The introduction of image-capture technology in *The Fellowship of the Ring* was another advance that altered the way films were made. All the way back in 1937, Disney first tried to capture the movement of actual people in animated form. In *Snow White and the Seven Dwarfs*, an actress was filmed making all the movements that were designed for Snow White. Animators then copied the film frames into the cartoon in an effort to make her character as lifelike as possible. Nearly 70 years later, Peter Jackson used computers and actor Andy Serkis to create the character Gollum for his *Lord of the Rings Trilogy*.

Interestingly, the other significant change of the 2000s dealt with the exact opposite kind of film, the documentary. For more than 100 years, documentary films had focused on giving audiences as "real" a look at real life as possible. The result was informative, sometimes eye-opening and thought-provoking films that rarely reached a large audience. Most documentaries didn't attempt to entertain, and most often wanted to focus on the material they were presenting as inconspicuously as possible.

That began to change with Michael Moore's 1989 film *Roger and Me*, in which the director was as much a part of the film as the subject matter. The film became the highest grossing documentary in history at the time, at $6.7 million. In 2002, Moore's *Bowling for Columbine* completely changed the way Hollywood looked at documentaries. The film was a critical and financial success, winning at the Cannes Film Festival and the Academy Awards in categories for which documentaries had never before been considered. The film made nearly $60 million, a total that would be dwarfed just two years later when *Fahrenheit 9/11* made more than $220 million. It is no longer expected that a documentary will lose money, as many turn at least a modest profit and some can make much more.

THE DEATH OF FILM?

Despite the success of the low-tech documentary films, most blockbusters are big money, big special-effect endeavors. Action-capture technology, digital cameras, and digital editing have given filmmakers the ability to do what they could never do before, but at what cost? In 2013, the film *Life of Pi* won four academy awards including one for Cinematography, yet the entire movie was filmed digitally and, with the exception of a few actors and a few props, nothing in the epic middle of the film existed in the real world. Does that alter our perception of the art form? Should it? Can we still call them films if they are not recorded on film or even projected on film in some cases? Before wringing our hands and decrying the end of motion pictures as we know it, we should remember that for all the advances in technology, there is still room for a good story and well-developed characters. The same year that *Life of Pi* won for Cinematography, the film *Argo*, a character-driven story with few special effects, won for Best Picture.

In many ways, movies today look very little like the first films of Melies and Lumiere, yet the elements that make up a movie—acting, directing, lighting, story, and so on—haven't changed in more than 100 years. The way we create movies and the way we use them have changed, but what makes a film remains. This book will look at those myriad elements and how they are synthesized into a coherent whole. Hundreds, sometimes thousands, of people work together toward one goal: creating a film. Now we will begin looking at what it is that they actually do to achieve that goal.

FILM LANGUAGE AND CRITICISM

CHAPTER 2

Cinema has a language all its own. It has its own vocabulary, and it gives different meanings to words that we already know. The sooner we are able to grasp this language, the sooner we will be able to understand the process of creating a film. This chapter will explore some of the general terms that will help you to develop the shorthand necessary to move through the world of film.

The Film Spectrum

Realism	Classicism	Formalism
Documentaries "Day in the life"	Most fiction films Standard story and narratives	Experimental Avant-garde

© Kendall Hunt Publishing Company

THE FILM SPECTRUM

First, let us look at what categories of films are made. It is helpful to think of these categories in a broad spectrum. At one end of the spectrum is **realism**, a style of filmmaking that seeks to present "life as it is" with little influence by the writer, director, actors, etc. Documentary films most commonly fit at this end of our spectrum. It is important to realize that there is no such thing as a 100% realistic film. The moment you turn on a camera and point it at people, it alters how they behave and how they react. To assume that "reality TV" is anything close to how the people involved in it would actually behave in "real life" is to be either in complete denial or utterly naïve.

A second reason why it is impossible to have a completely realistic film is that the simple act of pointing a camera at one subject rather than another is an editorial decision that alters what the audience can now know about whatever is being filmed. In other words, if I show children playing around a spraying fire hydrant but don't show the parents sitting on the porch looking miserable, I have altered the complete picture and it is therefore not "reality."

At the other end of the spectrum is **formalism**, a style of filmmaking in which aesthetic and artistic concerns are given a higher priority than capturing the "reality" of the situation. In the same way that it is not possible to have a 100% realistic film, it is not possible to have a 100% formalistic film. There must be some basis of both form and subject matter to consider it "real." For example, a film may consist of only colors and sounds and it may have no coherent story, yet the colors and sounds are "real" and therefore not completely formalistic. An avant-garde director is one who would lean far more toward formalism than realism.

Avant-garde is a way of making films that is abstract and experimental. It values technique over substance. While a documentarian would want to be subtle and unobtrusive, an avant-garde director would aim to be more outlandish, making the audience very aware of what was being done with editing, sound, camera angles, and so on.

The large center section of our spectrum is **classicism**, the area where most fiction films are found. They contain elements of realism and formalism blended together. Depending on the particular film, it may reside toward the realistic end of the spectrum like *Argo,* or it may drift toward the formalistic end like *Eraserhead.* It is important to remember that we are looking at a spectrum and, therefore, we are looking at degrees of realism and formalism. It is also important to realize that a film may fall along different areas of the spectrum in terms of its form or content.

Content is the material being shown in the film, the story. **Form** is how that story is told, the way in which it is presented. A film's content may be realistic, dealing with life as it is or was at a particular time; or it may be more formalistic, showing us a world with wizards and hobbits or aliens or talking sponges that wear a particular shape of pants. The same is true for form. If we present a story that deals with life as it is but do it in an animated form, the content is more realistic and the form is more formalistic.

SHOTS

Next, let us look at how the above-mentioned forms and styles are created. The name "motion pictures" is an accurate way to describe what is taking place when we watch a film. A modern film is presented at 24 frames per second, a **frame** being one still photographic image recorded on a filmstrip. If we do the math, we see that a typical two-hour film contains more than 170,000 images played one after another in rapid succession.

A shot is a collection of images that are recorded continuously from the time the camera begins running until it stops again, usually after the director says, "Cut." There are several ways to categorize what kind of shot we are looking at. The first explores the distance from the subject or how much of the subject the audience sees.

An **extreme long shot** is one taken at a great distance from the subject. It can be a shot of the vast countryside, a huge battle scene, even a shot of the earth from space. It gives the audience an omniscient view of the scene, allowing us to take in everything that is going on. It is often used as an **establishing shot**, a shot that tells the audience where we are and provides a greater context for later shots in the scene that will be closer to the action.

The second shot, which brings us closer, is the **long shot,** a shot that gives the audience a view of roughly what it would look like if the scene were being played out on the stage of an old-style "movie palace." This shot again gives us context and can be used as an establishing shot; however, the audience feels more connected to the scene as a result of being closer, and usually on the same level as the action.

This extreme long shot from Lord of the Rings: Return of the King gives a sense of the number of warriors heading out to battle while also providing an establishing shot of where they are and where they are headed.

Next we have a **full shot**. This type of shot is one in which we are able to see the full body of the subject with a small amount of space above the head and below the feet. This is often used as a **re-establishing shot**, which reminds the audience of the physical context of the scene after we have spent a significant amount of time in alternating shots that are much closer to the action.

A **medium shot** is a shot in which the subject, most often a person, is shown from the waist up or the knees up. This allows audiences to feel that they are more a part of the action, standing a few feet away and observing what is taking place in the scene.

As we continue to approach the subjects, we move into a **close-up shot**, a much more detailed look at the person or subject matter. At this distance we will see the actor from the shoulders or neck up only. This shot sacrifices context for detail, allowing us to better see and understand the feelings and reactions of the actor.

The final distance-oriented shot is an **extreme close-up**. This moves the audience to a distance that would be very uncomfortable in real life. It is an extremely detailed view of the subject. In terms of an actor, the entire shot might include only the eye or mouth, as in *Citizen Kane* when he utters "Rosebud."

Like an establishing shot or a re-establishing shot, a **master shot** is a long shot or extreme long shot. A master shot differs, however, because it films the entire scene in one continuous take. It is used in case the editing together of the parts of the scene run into continuity issues; that is, two shots that are going to be edited together don't match up.

There are other kinds of shots that may focus on the angle of the shot or what is contained in the shot. One such shot is called a **two shot**. As the name suggests, this is a shot in which two actors appear; this is almost always a medium shot. A **three shot** would have three actors, and so on, though once you get past three, the name used usually reverts to the distance from the subject.

14   Chapter 2

An **over-the-shoulder-shot** is a medium shot that is most often used when two actors are facing each other having a conversation. The shot is set up with the camera behind one actor looking into the face of the other. The shot is framed to include the shoulder and part of the head of the actor facing away from the camera to give the audience context.

A **point-of-view shot** (POV) moves the camera into the position of the character's body. It shows us what they see. It can be used in conjunction with an over-the-shoulder shot in a conversation scene to alter the audience's point of view. It can also be used as a a **cutaway shot,** a brief shot that interrupts the scene by showing something relating to the action in more detail. In terms of a POV shot, it shows us what the character is looking at—for example a note or a secret document. A **reaction shot** is a form of cutaway shot that shows how a character is reacting to the action of the scene or what another character has just done or said.

From 2003's Pirates of the Caribbean. Keira Knightley has just discovered that the pirates whose ship she shares are cursed and undead.

A shot that is making a comeback with the reintroduction of 3-D films is called a **head-on shot**. This is when the action or objects from the action come directly toward the camera to make the audience feel more involved in the story. These kinds of shots are often contrived and can seem out of place and stagey if done without properly motivating them in the story.

The angle of the shot can tell the audience a great deal about what is going on and pull the audience into the action. The most common angle is the **eye-level shot**. The camera is set at the eye level of the actors in the scene and gives audiences the feeling that they are standing next to the action. It is the most comfortable and "realistic" level from which to film a scene.

If we raise or lower the camera, we profoundly affect how the audience views the subject of the shot. A **high angle shot** looks down at the subject from a greater height. It causes the audience to see the subject as weak or in distress. This is not a conscious thought, but instinctively we know that if we are looking down at someone, that person is in trouble. The girl at the bottom of the well in *Silence of the Lambs* doesn't have to say a word. We know she is not in a position of power.

This high angle shot from Miller's Crossing shows us a man who could not be more weak and fragile. We look down on him as he begs for his life.

Conversely, a **low angle shot** looks up at the subject. This tells audiences that they are in control, in power. We do not worry about the subjects of low angle shots. In fact, we often fear them. One of the reasons that the character Darth Vader stands 7 feet tall is to give him that feeling of power and control.

This low angle shot from Pulp Fiction shows that, gun or no gun, actor John Travolta is in control of this situation.

Two other shots, which are used much less often, are the **oblique angle shot** and the **bird's-eye-view shot**. The oblique angle shot, sometimes called a dutch tilt, leans the camera to one side, giving the audience a disturbing, confusing, slanted view of the action. This shot tells the audience that something has gone terribly wrong; things are not as they should be. A Bird's-Eye-View shot is taken from directly above the action giving the audience a detached and omniscient point of view. In *It's A Wonderful Life*, we have this view just as George Bailey jumps into the river to drown himself. In this case, we are seeing a point-of-view shot from the eyes of the angel Clarence, who will be attempting to show George why his life is still worth living.

In the course of filming a movie, events can conspire against crews and force them to become more creative. For example, if the scene calls for rain and it is sunny outside, lenses, filters, and camera effects (along with a big hose and lots of water) can be used to make it rain. In the 1950s and 1960s, the lighting technology was not good enough to film well outdoors at night, so cinematographers developed a **day-for-night shot**. This again used filters and lenses to make it seem like it was nighttime while filming in bright sunlight. If you ever see a film from this period and wonder why everything seems to be taking place during a super-bright full moon, this is why. Technology today has developed to a point at which this kind of shot is rarely, if ever, used.

There are more kinds of shots and certainly more cinema-specific vocabulary that will be covered in this text as we go through the different elements that make up a film, but this should give us a solid starting point from which we can build.

THEORY AND CRITICISM

Anyone who has ever watched a film has had an opinion about it. Theory and criticism are two ways that films can be analyzed and evaluated. Next we will look at the ways in which film analysts evaluate the success or lack of success that any film might achieve.

Criticism is a broad term used to describe how film experts try to determine the relative value of any given film. There are two primary categories for this kind of film evaluator: reviewer and critic.

REVIEWER

A **reviewer** is an individual who describes the film, looking at its overall content and tone while attempting to categorize it. Reviewers rarely evaluate the elements that make up the film. A reviewer will often discuss whether the film is appropriate for certain age groups and draw parallels to other films that are more widely known ("If you liked *The Avengers*, you'll love Iron Man 3.")

CRITIC

Unlike a reviewer, a **critic** looks very closely at the elements that make up the film and attempts to determine how well those elements were incorporated to create a successful motion picture. Greek philosopher Aristotle outlined the basic elements of criticism nearly 2,500 years ago by essentially asking: 1) What were they trying to accomplish? 2) Did they succeed? 3) Why or why not? It is in the second and third questions that critics spend most of their time. Still, it is important to first look at what the artist, in this case the filmmaker, was trying to accomplish. In general terms, it can be assumed that all filmmakers are attempting to create a good-quality movie. In specific terms however, is it honest to say that Michael Bay was trying to accomplish the same thing with *Transformers* 3 that Benh Zeitlin was trying to do with *Beasts of the Southern Wild*? Truly great films will be able achieve both the general and specific goals equally well, but it is important to keep in mind that there is a place for well-made movies that are ultimately just trying to entertain an audience.

FILM THEORY AND CRITICISM

Film theory is a vast subject that has many texts devoted solely to its study. In this text we are going to take a brief look at it in terms of how it is used in film criticism. In addition to film reviewers and critics, film theorists also analyze film. Theorists take the time to explore specific elements of a movie at great length. While there is some evaluation, often a theorist is analyzing the film to determine themes and messages that may not be easily identified in a single viewing. For our purposes, we will be looking at film theory for its evaluative function. While there are myriad elements that a critic can analyze, they basically fall into three components:, the artist, the audience, and the film as a work of art.

THE ARTIST

If critics want to analyze a film's value by looking at an individual artist, they will most often look at the work of the director. In later chapters we will discuss the role and function of the director, but for the purpose of criticism, it is the director's job to create the film by bringing all of the disparate elements of cinema together into a single cohesive work of art. It is therefore reasonable for a critic to praise or criticize directors for any of the elements in the film since, ostensibly, they are the individuals who approved all of those choices. In this form of cinematic criticism, each of the elements of film—acting, lighting, sound, editing, cinematography, etc.—are evaluated for what they were trying to achieve and how successful they were at achieving it.

This is the form of criticism found in most college film classes. It is an analysis that goes further than what you might find in the newspaper or on most websites, though not as far as the more esoteric theory analysis you might find in film theory textbooks and research papers.

AUDIENCE

If critics want to evaluate a film by looking at the way it will be received by an audience, the focus will be less specific than the analysis done when looking at the work of individual elements of a film. The primary analysis will still be on the work and decisions of the director, but the question will be asked in more general terms. It will be focused on what the directors were trying to achieve in the audience's reaction to the film as much as it is about what they were trying to achieve artistically. Many of your more well-known critics and virtually all reviewers will find themselves using this style of analysis to evaluate the film's relative value.

WORK OF ART

If critics are looking at the film in terms of its function as a work of art, they will focus more on its overall narrative and where it falls on the spectrum of realism to formalism. Many individual critics and theorists believe that film should be either realistic or formalistic, that it is a function of film to be one or the other and it should not, therefore, ever be the other. In simpler terms, theorists who believe that film should be realistic speak out against films that make their way toward the formalistic end of the spectrum. The opposite is true for theorists who believe that film should be formalistic. While there is certainly a place for this discussion in an overall analysis of film, it is less helpful in evaluating the quality of an individual film.

Looking back at Aristotle's three questions, a critic can ask what the film was trying to achieve in terms of its narrative. Was it trying to be realistic, formalistic, somewhere in between? How successful was it? Why or why not? Truthfully, this way of looking at individual films and evaluating the value as a work of art lends itself more to the realm of theorists rather than reviewers or critics.

OVERVIEW

The website Rotten Tomatoes, www.rottentomatoes.com, takes a composite look at all the major outlets' reviews and critiques for each film and compiles a rating based on the percentage of those reviews that are positive and negative. It also allows website members to rate how they felt about the film. Rotten Tomatoes rates a film as "certified fresh" if it receives at least 60% positive ratings from critics. This group of critics tends to analyze in terms of either the artist or the audience, so there is a slight difference between critic ratings and audience ratings for the best films. The largest disparity in ranking comes in the films that were panned by critics but still found an audience. For example, *Avatar*, the highest grossing film of all time, received a critics' ranking of 89% and an audience ranking of 92%—fairly close. But Eddie Murphy's 2012 box-office bomb *A Thousand Words* got a critics' ranking of 0% and a 48% audience ranking.

When evaluating the relative worth of a film, it is important to remember that all the opinions, no matter how educated, are just opinions. If viewers are looking for a silly, light-hearted comedy, they might be well entertained by a film that critics revile as "a whole lot of nothing." The value of a film is, at least to a point, relative.

Review

Take the following vocabulary list and define each term in your own words to make sure that you understand film language:

Realism

Classicism

Formalism

Avant-Garde

Content

Form

Frame

Establishing Shot

Re-establishing Shot

Extreme Long Shot

Long Shot

Full Shot

Medium Shot

Close-up Shot

Extreme Close-up

Master Shot

Two Shot

Three Shot

Over-the-shoulder Shot

Head-on Shot

Point-of-view Shot

Cutaway Shot

Reaction Shot

Eye-level Shot

High angle Shot

Low angle Shot

Oblique angle Shot

Bird's-eye-view Shot

Day-for-night Shot

Reviewer

Critic

MISE-EN-SCENE

CHAPTER 3

Film is a visual medium. It is more about images than words. If you think about your favorite movies, even if you remember quotes from them, it is the visual image that stays with you. The French term *mise-en-scene* refers to the visual design aspects of film or play. For our purposes, mise-en-scene has to do with every part of an image that appears on a frame of film. If film is a visual medium, the visual elements that make up shot or scene are the most important aspects of the film.

The old saying, "Every picture tells a story" is particularly true in film. Each shot is set up by the director and cinematographer (or director of photography) to tell part of the overall story of the film. The premise is that a well designed film allows you to pull out virtually any single frame and understand what is going on, at least on some level, whether you have seen the film before or not. In this chapter we are going to explore all the elements that make up mise-en-scene and how directors and cinematographers use them to convey the film's vision.

12 ELEMENTS OF MISE-EN-SCENE

We will take the image above and use the 12 different elements that make up mise-en-scene to analyze what is going on in the scene. What are the relationships? What is the message? What is important?

1. **Primary Focus/Dominant**

    Look at the image above. What is the first thing that you notice? That is called the dominant. Wherever our eyes go first should be the most important part of the image. Most likely you focused on the character's (Ofelia's) face. We are drawn to it for a number of reasons; it is near the center of the frame, and it belongs to the only visible person in the shot. If this is the most important part of the image, what does it tell us? It tells us that Ofelia is the most important thing in this shot. We therefore connect with her, and she becomes our entry point into the shot. As we look at other elements, we will begin to get a clearer image of what is happening.

2. **Lighting Key**

    The lighting key deals with the source of the light in the scene. There are three primary choices of lighting key: **high key** lighting, **low key** lighting and **high contrast** lighting. High key is used predominantly in comedies and musicals. High key lighting has very little shadow and lots and lots of light. Low key is often used in mysteries or horror films, and uses very little light with lots of shadows. The third kind, high contrast lighting, has to do with large differences in brightness between the dark and light elements in the scene. Film noir movies like *The Maltese Falcon* and *Touch of Evil* make extensive use of this kind of lighting. We sometimes have what is called **moderate key** lighting, which is a sort of middle ground between high key and low key.

Returning to our image from above, what kind of lighting key are we looking at? The most accurate description would be high contrast lighting. Ofelia's face and the pools of light are very bright while the ceiling and shadows on the left side of the image are very dark. This kind of contrast, particularly used in this way, sets up a suspenseful mood in which we are concerned for the subject, Ofelia.

3. Color

The next element to look at is the use of color in the image. Is there a dominant color like the recurring red in *Run, Lola, Run*? Is there a symbolic color like Hamlet's black costume, which shows both that he is in mourning and that he stands apart from the rest of the citizens of Denmark in Kenneth Branagh's opening scene of *Hamlet*? In our shot the primary colors are red and green. Red can signify love, anger, danger or blood or it can be a warning to stop. In this case, the red on the paintings seem to be a bloody and dangerous warning. Ofelia's light green coat, on the other hand, makes her look young, somewhat optimistic, and innocent. The contrast between her clothing and the large swaths of red paint shows that she is out of place and in danger.

4. Secondary Focus

If the dominant is where the eye looks first, the subsidiary contrast or secondary focus is where the eye looks next. If Ofelia's face is where we look first, what else in this frame catches our eye—the paintings along the corridor, the columns, pools of light, perhaps the light fixtures above? Each of these catches our attention if we look long enough. The columns and pools of light lead us down the corridor much the same way they lead Ofelia down the corridor. Like her, we feel a pull to see what is waiting at the end.

5. Density

Density is the amount of visual information in a frame. It is often thought of as how much "stuff" is present (tables, books, knickknacks, etc.), but our example illustrates how that is not necessarily the case. There are paintings and columns along the hallway, but not much else. Still, the size of the paintings and the closeness of the columns give the scene a very dense feeling. The corridor is almost stifling, and the only truly open space is heading down the center of the hall. This adds to the pull to go further. It is the only place to go.

6. Composition

The composition of the scene focuses on dividing up the space. It can greatly affect how we "feel" in the space. There are a number of ways that the environment can be arranged, and each choice alters our view. The three primary elements of composition are **line, mass, texture,** and the way in which they are used together creates a fourth, **balance.**

Line is the outline of the elements in the scene. Are most of the lines leading our eyes vertically, horizontally, or diagonally? Vertical lines suggest an uplifting and positive feeling. The longer the lines, the more open, free, and uplifted we feel. Horizontal lines suggest stability and calm. The longer the line, the safer and more stable we feel. Diagonal lines can be exciting and dynamic but can also cause anxiety, as illustrated in an oblique angle shot.

Mass is the size and perceived weight of an object. For example, a stone statue, even a small one, has more mass than a large stuffed animal.

The feel of items is their **texture**. If we are looking at a room that has soft fabric couches, it has a different feel than a room with stiff wooden chairs. Texture can convey the comfort and warmth, or lack thereof, of a space.

Balance means that the mass on both sides of the scene is the same. In almost all cases, we want to establish a balance where each side of the scene has the perceived weight because the audience will notice the imbalance and feel that something is wrong in the scene. There are two ways to achieve balance: **symmetrically** and **asymmetrically**. In symmetrical balance, the items on both sides are the same in shape, height, weight, number, etc. Asymmetrical balance has items that are the same in total perceived weight or mass but are different in size, number, etc. For example, if you have 25 folding chairs on one side and a grand piano on the other, you have roughly achieved asymmetrical balance.

In our scene the composition tells us much about this hidden corridor that Ofelia has discovered. In terms of line, we have the vertical lines of the columns that would make us feel uplifted, but this is broken up and cut short by the poles leading down the corridor. The paintings add to the horizontal feel, which would seem to add comfort and stability, but it is offset by the curve at the end of the hall. The chief feeling is again that of being led down to an unknown end.

The texture of the columns seems rough, and the floor is stone, which is also rough and uneven. The balance of the scene is symmetrical with columns and paintings on both sides matching left and right perfectly. What offsets the balance again is the curve at the end of the hall, which adds mass to the right side of the screen and makes the audience feel anxious.

7. Form

Form is the most difficult element of mise-en-scene to describe and analyze. The form can either be open or closed. An open form is one where there is no obvious framing inside the boundaries of the shot. That is, there are no arches, doorways or other such constraints that seem to limit the movement of the characters. A closed form is the opposite; there are frames or barriers apparent in the shot that provide a frame-within-a-frame. If a character is framed standing inside a doorway, this character will seem trapped, contained, or hindered in some way. A closed form can also assist in establishing balance in a shot; the area inside of the framing element (door, arch, window, etc.) will be viewed as its own space and, as such, the objects inside it should maintain a sense of balance as well.

In our example, we have an extremely closed form. There are framing elements throughout the shot: The columns, the walls, the frames, and the hallway all act as barriers to Ofelia. Once again, it feels as though the only choice she has is to continue down the hall.

8. **Framing**

    While framing sounds very similar to form, these two are actually quite different. Form looks at elements inside the shot that might contain the characters and the action inside them, whereas framing looks at where on the frame the character or subject is. Does that character have the ability to move around the space freely or not? If a character appears near the edge of the frame or if the shot is a close-up where there is very little open space beyond the edge of the subject, we have what is called tight framing. Loose framing occurs when the camera is farther away or there is open space in which the character can move around. The similarity in framing and form is the feeling it gives the audience. Tight framing, like closed form, makes the character appear trapped or blocked. Loose framing is more like open form; it suggests freedom and possibilities.

    Returning to Ofelia in the hallway we may be confused at first because it is clearly a loosely framed shot. Doesn't this contradict the closed form that we looked at just moments ago? Not at all. If you remember that closed form was driving her down the hall, the loose framing, then, gives her the ability to move down the hall. If this shot was tightly framed we wouldn't be able to see down the hall and the scene would have an entirely different feel and message. She needs to be able to move, but the closed form gives her only one direction in which to move.

9. **Depth**

    Our eyes allow us to see relatively clearly things that are close to us or far away (as long as we are not near-sighted or far-sighted). Lenses in the camera can allow us to do the same thing. Depending on what kind of lens we are using, we can either see one distance clearly while the rest is out of focus or we can see all the distances clearly simultaneously. The more distances we can see clearly, the greater is the depth of field of the shot. When analyzing a frame, the objects that are in focus are most important, while those that are out of focus have no real value. A shot with a small depth of field tells us that only one plane (distance) has important information on it. Conversely, a large depth of field, or **deep-focus shot**, tells us that much of the shot is important and that we need to be aware of additional objects or the spatial relationship of objects inside the frame.

    In the shot from *Pan's Labyrinth*, we can see clearly all the way down the long corridor. The purpose of this deep-focus shot is not to allow us to see all of the columns clearly but, rather to see the length and, in this case, emptiness of the corridor. If the only plane in focus was the one in which Ofelia is contained, the corridor would not seem as foreboding and intimidating. By being able to see all the way down the corridor, it tells us that Ofelia has a long way to go and, judging from the design of the hall, anything might happen to her along the way.

10. **Character Placement**

    Where on the frame do we find the subject or subjects? Each part of the screen tells a little something different about the subject that is occupying it. For example, the top of the frame suggests power, strength, joy, glory, and the like. Subjects at the bottom of the screen are seen as weak, inferior, and vulnerable. This echoes the idea behind high angle and low angle shots. We look down (physically, in this case) on those who are weak and look up at those who are strong. The same is true for their placement in the frame. Objects that appear at the edges of the frame are seen as insignificant because of their distance from the center of the frame. They tend to be in our peripheral vision and, as such, are not points of focus for the audience.

    In our shot, we see that Ofelia is slightly above the center of the frame, giving her some power but not a great deal, and she is slightly off to the side, weakening her somewhat. She is clearly the most significant object in the shot, but she is by no means in control of the situation.

11. Staging Position

The character can appear in any of five basic staging positions in relationship to the camera: full-front, quarter right or left, profile, three-quarter right or left, and full-back. We relate to characters in relation to how much we can see their face and, to a lesser degree, the front of their body. The more they are facing the camera, the stronger they appear.

Full-front is when the actor is facing directly into the camera. This is the strongest position and shows confidence while providing a way for the audience to connect with the character. The way we feel about that character effects how we interpret the body position. If the hero of a piece is facing directly at us, we feel positively toward the hero. A villain in the same position feels intimidating or threatening. This is why, in a film when the villain is first beaten back, though by no means completely defeated, the villain will often back away rather than turning to go. By backing away, the villain remains facing the camera and continues to have power and convey danger.

A **quarter turn** right or left is a comfortable way for the audience to view a character. It is not as confrontational as full-front, yet it allows us to see the character clearly and still make a connection. This is the most common staging position used in film.

A **profile** turn is a side view of the character. It gives the audience less of a connection to the action, almost as if the character is unaware that we are there or is ignoring us. This position is used most often in two-shots and gives equal significance to both characters in the shot. A character in profile evokes a fairly neutral feeling in the audience, seeming neither weak nor strong. As the character continues to look more away from the audience, the strength or power continues to diminish.

Once we reach a **three-quarter** turn right or left, the character has very little perceived power or significance to the audience. Usually a character in this position is providing secondary focus by turning to look at the dominant or primary focus of the shot.

A character facing **full-back**, turned to look directly away from the camera, rarely has any significance for the audience. The most common use of full-back is in crowd scenes, where individual members of the crowd have no significance. Only in that they are part of a crowd has importance. The one exception to this rule is if a single person attempts to hide the identity or some object being held in their possession by looking away. Then the position conveys a sense of mystery and suspense.

Ofelia standing in the corridor is interesting because she gives us two contradictory staging positions. Her body is in a three-quarter right position, giving us the idea that she is weak or unimportant. Her face, however, is looking back at us in a one-quarter turn with her eyes looking almost full-front. We perceive power and importance from the face of a character, so, despite her body position, Ofelia has significance and is in a position in which we can relate to her and feel for her. We are concerned for her well-being.

12. Distance

When we talk about distance in mise-en-scene, we are talking about distance between characters. The way that we use distance in real life is divided into four categories. The first category, **intimate space,** is from physical contact to 18 inches away. The people we allow into this distance are our significant others, immediate family, and close friends. This distance conveys love, intimacy, and tenderness. The next distance, called **personal space,** is from 18 inches to 4 feet away. This distance is reserved for our friends and acquaintances, people with whom we are familiar and comfortable. From 4 to 12 feet away, the distance is called **social distance**. In our everyday lives we allow pretty much anyone who doesn't have a restraining order against to enter this space. This is called social distance because it usually occurs in social situations like parties and events. Beyond 12 feet is what we call **public distance**. This is a more formal distance that we usually experience at sporting events, concerts, and public viewing of films. This is a distance between us and the subject of our attention, the performer. This is not to say that you would have a distance of 12 or more feet between you and the nearest audience member.

Ofelia is completely alone in this shot; there is no distance to analyze. The fact that there is no one else in this shot tells us something. It tells us that she is alone and isolated. The look on our face tells us that she is worried, if not downright frightened.

CAMERA

Before we end our analysis of the scene from *Pan's Labyrinth*, we should look at the primary tool for creating the mise-en-scene—the camera. The camera uses a number of elements to set up the shot and the cinematographer makes decisions with the camera that, while not technically part of the mise-en-scene, can be used to analyze what is going on in a given frame of film.

SHOT

In the previous chapter we talked about the different kinds of shots. In this case, we are talking about the distance of the camera from the action: extreme long shot, long shot, full shot, medium shot, close-up, extreme close-up. We judge the distance of the shot from the dominant because it is the true subject of the shot. In our example, we are looking at a medium shot of Ofelia. We see from roughly the waist up, which keeps us at a distance. We are not as connected as we would be in a close-up, but what the medium shot allows us to see is the full length and width of the corridor, which is very important to this scene.

CAMERA ANGLE

In the last chapter we talked about the different camera angles: high angle, low angle, oblique angle, bird's-eye-view, and eye level. Choosing any one of those angles tells the audience something specific about the subject of the shot. For Ofelia we find ourselves at eye level, which is a comfortable position for us to be in, but notice that she is looking slightly above the camera, making it feel like a slightly high angle shot in that we feel she is in a weakened position. We feel connected to her, but we are worried that she might be in trouble.

LENS

We talked about depth of field above. The depth of field in a shot is dependent upon the kind of lens that is used. The most common types of lenses are **telephoto** and **wide-angle** lenses. A telephoto lens gives the audience a closer view of the elements of the shot. The cost is that the shot loses its sense of depth. It means that objects are clearly visible on only one plane while anything in front of or behind that plane becomes fuzzy and insignificant. A wide-angle lens gives more depth, allowing items on any plane to be seen clearly. The drawback is that even subjects in the foreground seem farther away. The depth of field in our shot means that we are clearly using a wide-angle lens. The use of that lens also makes the corridor seem longer and more forbidding than it would have if the director had used a telephoto lens.

FILTER

If directors or cinematographers want to add color to a scene without using a specific object in that color, they can use filters. Filters can be subtle, as in the rain sequence from *Four Weddings and a Funeral*, where a slightly blue filter was added to make the rain seem colder, or they can be more obvious like the red filter used in the pillow scenes from *Run, Lola, Run*. Our shot uses the red from the paintings rather than using a filter to serve the purpose.

Filters were also used in the 1940s and 1950s to turn daytime shots into to nighttime shots because the lighting was not good enough to shoot effectively outdoors at night in locations where lights were not already present. Westerns used this method fairly often because they would be filming out on the plains or in the desert with no built-in light source available. This meant that all of the lighting had to be provided by the film crew. It also meant that the lighting would have to look like it was moonlight since there would be no electric light sources on the plains.

Film Stock

The rapidly changing way in which movies are "filmed" is making this element less important every day. Digital cameras are increasingly being used in the movie-making process, which means that the kind of film, or **film stock**, is becoming less of a decision for directors and cinematographers. If filmmakers decide to use film rather than digital technology, they need to decide what film stock they will use.

Fast stock film is used most often in documentary- type films or films that attempt to be as "real" as possible. Fast stock does not require much additional lighting, which means that the filming process can be done more quickly and, in the case of documentary films, less obtrusively. The primary drawback, if you even choose to look at it that way, is that the film looks very rough and grainy. In *Run, Lola, Run*, the scenes between her father and his mistress are recorded on fast stock film to give it that gritty, realistic look.

Slow stock film is used for the vast majority of mainstream films. While it does require significantly more lighting to use slow stock, the end result is a much clearer and more professional-looking image.

Digital recording presents a high-definition image that is even clearer than slow stock film while requiring less, though not significantly less, illumination from outside sources.

FINAL ANALYSIS

After having looked at the 12 elements of mise-en-scene and the ways in which the camera was used to set up the image of Ofelia in the corridor, we can draw some fairly clear conclusions. First and foremost, almost everything in the shot is pulling us and Ofelia to go down the hallway—the depth of field, the balance of composition, the lighting, and so forth. We know that she is out of place, and we worry for her safety Yet, like Ofelia, we are intrigued and want to see what is waiting at the end of the hallway.

Review

The 12 elements of mise-en-scene are:

1. Dominant
2. Lighting Key
3. Color
4. Cecondary Focus
5. Density

6. Composition
7. Form
8. Framing
9. Depth
10. Character Placement
11. Staging Positions
12. Distance

The parts of the camera and the way they are used are integral to creating the mise-en-scene. The shot, angles, lens, filters, and film stock can each dramatically alter the images in any scene.

EDITING

CHAPTER 4

Editing, in its most basic sense, is the joining of one strip of film to another strip of film that was recorded at a different time. Today, virtually all editing is done digitally, even in movies that are shot on film.

An average 2-hour film actually has 20–40 hours of footage that is filmed. The additional footage includes outtakes, additional shots of scenes from different angles, scenes that didn't make the final film, and the like. It is the job of the editor, in conjunction with the director, to decide which 2 hours of footage will be used to tell the story in the best possible way.

No editing to see here, the entire film Arrival of a Train is one shot.

In the earliest days of film, the movie was one continuous shot. *Arrival of a Train* started with the train beginning to pull in and ended when everyone had disembarked from the train. The film was 15 minutes long, and the shot was 15 minutes long because the event was 15 minutes long. It didn't take filmmakers long to realize the advantage of editing in the process of telling a story. By the early 1900s, they had developed the most basic form of editing, cutting to continuity.

CUTTING TO CONTINUITY

Cutting to continuity is the process of condensing the recorded time of an event. This method of editing allows us to take out the "unnecessary" sections of an event.

For example, if we want to tell part of a story in which a woman leaves her office and drives home, we probably don't want to show every second of the 25–30-minute journey from her office to her home. Instead of one continuous 30-minute shot, we might have something that looks more like this:

1. She exits her office, turns back, and locks the door. She then heads down the hall toward the elevators. **(CUT)**
2. She walks up to the elevator, presses the button, the doors open, she enters the elevator and turns back to face the camera as the doors close. **(CUT)**
3. On the ground floor the doors open, she walks out of the elevator, says goodnight to the receptionist at the front desk, and exits through front door into the parking lot. **(CUT)**
4. In the parking lot she walks to her car, gets in, starts the car, and drives out onto the roadway, narrowly missing a young boy on a bicycle. **(CUT)**
5. Inside the car she reacts to the near accident. She checks her mirror to see if the boy is okay, and takes a few deep breaths. She continues driving toward her home. **(CUT)**
6. She drives down her street and into the driveway of her house. **(CUT)**
7. She exits her car and walks up to her front door. She drops her keys just as she reaches the door, so she crouches down to pick them up. **(CUT)**
8. While crouching down, she notices that her front door is slightly ajar. Someone has broken into her house. **(CUT)**

This is an extremely simplistic sequence, particularly in terms of modern editing techniques, but it illustrates the time compression element of cutting to continuity. A 30-minute trip home has become a 2- to 3-minute scene. This kind of editing gives us a simple way to move the story along. The audience members understand that they have been given only the pertinent information and that the rest of the time has been edited out.

In a scene like this, it is likely that all the movement in the sequence would be in the same direction. If she moves from right to left across the scene down the hall to begin with and then we see her traveling left to right walking up to the elevator, it will confuse the audience. We will instinctively think she has turned around to go back to her office, so when she arrives at the elevator instead, the audience will feel that something is wrong.

DIRECTOR'S LINE

The premise behind this audience reaction is called the **director's line**, a line that divides the scene into two 180-degree angles. Once the camera is set on one side of the line, it can't be moved to the other side. For example, if we have a two-shot where Jack is on the left side of the screen and Al is on the right side, we have established that we are shooting on this side of the actors who, in this case, represent the director's line. We can't now move the camera to the other side of the actors for the next shot. If we do, Jack will suddenly appear on the right side of the screen and Al will be on the left. It will appear to the audience that the two characters suddenly, for no apparent reason, switched sides in the middle of their conversation. The audience members may not consciously understand why things seem wrong, but they will instinctively know that something is not right in the scene. This will distract them from the action of the scene, which is the last thing that you want to do.

JUMP CUT

Another editing "mistake" is called a **jump cut**. Technically, a jump cut is an edit that moves us from one distance from the subject to another without changing the angle. If we are looking at Jack in profile from a medium shot and we then cut to a long shot of Jack in profile, it will disrupt the audience members' attention. They will feel that they have suddenly "jumped" back several feet from the action, which will be very disconcerting to them and again take their attention away from the action of the scene. The original definition has grown so that jump cut is often used to describe any kind of editing choice that is confusing in terms of space and time.

While this is technically a poor choice in editing, it can be used for a specific purpose in a more formalist approach to a film. In *Run, Lola, Run*, we see Lola running away from us. She is a few feet away when suddenly she "jumps" to a distance of 10 or more feet from us. Director Tom Twyker is not making a mistake. This film is more toward the formalist end of the spectrum in its presentation, and he wants the audience to be continually aware that they are watching a film.

CLASSICAL CUTTING

The second primary style of editing is called **classical cutting**. While this style was developed by many filmmakers over time in the first decade and a half of the 20th century it was the director D.W. Griffith who took what many other directors were doing, put it all together, and expanded on it. In his 1915 film *The Birth of a Nation*, he used classical cutting in a way that would completely alter how films were to be made afterward. Classical cutting involves using editing to show an emotional or psychological connection.

For example, the early Russian filmmakers were experimenting with the process by juxtaposing a shot of an expressionless actor with a variety of other shots. **Juxtaposition** means to place one thing next to another, which essentially describes the process of editing. In this case, they showed audience members the shot of the actor, followed by a shot of a bowl of soup, and asked them what they thought the actor was feeling. The audience said he looked hungry. Then they showed a different audience the shot of the actor, followed by a shot of a beautiful young girl. The audience said he was in love. A third audience, shown the actor followed by a shot of a bed, said he looked tired. Even though the actor never saw the bowl of soup, the girl, or the bed, the audience believed he was looking at each of those items. The filmmakers realized that through editing, they could get the audience to perceive things in a different way. It could show what someone was feeling or thinking about at the time.

Griffith took editing a step further by showing action taking place at multiple locations simultaneously. Prior to this, most films showed events chronologically and didn't really explore the idea of simultaneous action. This process, called **parallel editing**, which shows action at multiple locations, proved to be an effective way of building suspense. It has since become a staple of action films and thrillers while being used in some form or another in most movies.

With the advent of classical cutting, editing became more prevalent and more useful. This new editing also required new kinds of shots. We mentioned establishing shots and re-establishing shots earlier in the text; they are crucial to the editing process once you start using the classical cutting. An establishing shot works well as a transition from one location to the next. It lets the audience know where the action is taking place. A re-establishing shot is effective not only as a transition but, if showing simultaneous action, it can be used to make those transitions between locations smoother.

Pacing

Now that we had these new editing techniques and shots, directors could do more with just the way the film was edited. For example, if they wanted a scene to seem fast-paced, perhaps for a car-chase scene, they would use more cuts. The shorter you stay with an image, the faster it makes that action feel to the audience. On the other end, if directors want to slow down the action, they will stay with each shot longer and have fewer cuts. This is often used for very dramatic or romantic scenes.

The use of editing for the purpose of pacing changed dramatically with the birth of MTV. Music videos began using shots that were only one or two seconds long, much faster than you saw in almost any film. As a result, audiences began to get used to the increased number of edits so now audiences often struggle with movies made prior to MTV. Films made at that time used so few edits by comparison that they seem to be very slow and boring to modern audiences.

In the 1950s, Alfred Hitchcock was considered borderline crazy for having 600–700 shots in a movie. The average film at the time had somewhere in the neighborhood of 250–350 shots, and today an action film might have 2,000 or more shots. Most of the time, when audiences today say they find old films boring, it has more to do with the sense of pacing established by the editing than with the story or the acting.

Prior to the age of MTV, watching the slow trek of camels across the desert sand as the sun slowly sets in this scene from Lawrence of Arabia, was a perfectly acceptable pace for a film.

Columbia Pictures / Photofest

DIRECTOR'S THUMBPRINT

How directors choose to use the editing in a film can say a lot about directors and what they are trying to achieve in the film. We mentioned earlier Tom Twyker's desire for the audience members to be aware that they are watching a film. Directors who want to the audience to be aware of their presence are said to have left a large thumbprint. That is, we can identify them from their style of editing or storytelling. This would be a film that resides more toward the formalist end of our spectrum. The director is trying to be more stylized and, by definition, less realistic. **Avant-garde** directors are those who try to experiment and make their film in a different way. This kind of director would leave a large thumbprint and use editing techniques that would draw the audience's attention to them. They would use a large number of edits, incorporating seemingly bad choices like jump cuts and "heavy-handed" editing choices.

Directors who wish to be more subtle and less visible to the audience would leave a small thumbprint and try to be more realistic in the way they present the content of the film. The more "real" directors are trying to be, the more likely they would use less obvious editing techniques and fewer shots. The smaller number does not mean back to the 250 or so from the 1940s and 1950s but, rather, that in the same kind of scene, they would use fewer edits than an avant-garde director might use.

In order to save time and money, directors will often use a process called **storyboarding,** in which the director draws a rough sketch of each shot ahead of time. It allows directors to more clearly and accurately convey their vision. This allows the cinematographer to set up the shots more quickly and keeps the filming process moving. The less time spent on a set with 50–100 people standing around getting paid, the more money is saved.

MASTER SHOTS AND CONTINUITY

One of the reasons that there is so much extra footage shot for a film is to help in the editing process. The more choices a director and editor have, the more likely they are to be able to put together the best possible film. The biggest problem in the editing process is having shots that you wish to put together but they don't match up. When you film a scene multiple times from multiple angles, things can change. The actors could be in different positions, or the lines could be said differently, or any of a number of differences can occur. There may not be a usable version of a scene from a particular angle.

To handle these kinds of problems, a director may use a master shot. A **master shot**, sometimes called a cover shot, is a long shot of the scene from beginning to end. A master shot is often used in epic scenes, like the battle scenes of *The Lord of the Rings,* as re-establishing shots that let the audience see what is going on in the battle as a whole. In the editing process, this kind of shot allows the director and editor to fill in any holes that may have occurred in the filming that may have required them to go back much later and re-shoot the scenes—a process that is very time-consuming and expensive.

The major drawback of a master shot has to do with the director's vision. The director puts together the film with the aid of the editor and turns it into the production company. This is called the **first cut** of the film. The **final cut** of the film is the one that is seen by audiences in theaters. Very few directors get the right to control the final cut; that is entirely the right of the production company. So, once the director turns in the first cut of the film, producers may decide that they don't like a scene or section of the film and want to "fix" it. If there are master shots for every scene available, the producer can go back and make massive changes to the way the film is put together, altering and even destroying the director's vision of the film.

Other changes from take to take (a **take** refers to each different time the scene is shot) that can make editing difficult is when the actors' work changes, or a prop is different or in a different place. These are called **errors in continuity**. Clocks are the most common culprits in continuity errors because a scene is being shot over

36 Chapter 4

The famous shower scene from Psycho as it was originally storyboarded by director Alfred Hitchcock.

a period of hours so, unless the clock is unplugged or the battery taken out, the clock will keep running. The result is a scene in which one shot shows the time as 6:32, then 10:15, then 5:47, then 10:15 again, and so on. This is especially difficult with digital clocks, as they can't be stopped and must be reset at the start of each shot.

The other most common continuity error has to do with food, drinks, and cigarettes. The level of the drink or cigarette and the amount and kind of food have to be watched and reset for each take; otherwise the drink may go from full to empty to half full, and so on. One of the more egregious examples of this can be found in the 2001 re-make of *Ocean's Eleven*. In a scene where Matt Damon is talking to Brad Pitt as Julia Roberts walks down a broad staircase, Pitt is eating shrimp cocktail. As the shots go back and forth, the container of Pitt's shrimp cocktail changes from a bowl to a plate and back several times.

Any number of people from props to costume to director to editor should be looking for continuity errors. Yet, in film after film, they can be found, sometimes as many as 10 to 12 in one film.

MONTAGE

The early Russian experiments in juxtaposition developed into a way of shooting and editing a sequence called a **montage**. This process involved taking fragments of a scene and piecing them together to create a unified sequence of events. Their use of montage was to build emotional connection to the events. This thematic form of editing was in full display in the 1925 film *Battleship Potemkin*, in which director Sergei Eisenstein used montage to show the scene of the Tsar's army slaughtering a group of protesting peasants on the Odessa Steps. This sequence is still widely regarded as one of the greatest uses of montage in cinematic history. It is so well regarded that it has been echoed in sequences from films like *The Untouchables* more than 50 years later.

Montage can also be used as a way to compress a large amount of time into a very short period. In cutting to continuity, we might compress 30 minutes into 3 minutes. In montage we are more likely to compress 30 days into 3 minutes. The most common version of this kind of montage is the training sequence. For example, in the film *Rocky* we see the final several weeks of his training for a title fight against Apollo Creed in a 3-minute sequence. This shows us how he is improving—getting faster, stronger, and better until he appears to be ready for the fight. We then pick up the action on the day before the title bout. Unlike the Odessa Steps sequence, this type of montage is usually accompanied by up-tempo, inspirational music to get the audience excited to see what happens next.

MODERN EDITING

With the introduction of digital editing into the filmmaking process, the editing of a film now occurs much more quickly and allows for much greater flexibility. Originally, editing involved taking sections of filmstrips, identifying the exact frame to begin and end the shot and physically taping them to another strip of film. Once a shot was cut, changing their mind was much more costly and time-consuming. With today's technology you can edit a scene together, undo the edit, and put it together in an entirely different way in a matter of a few minutes. This flexibility results in a higher quality of editing and a final product that more closely resembles the overall director's vision.

When we examine the editing of a film, we can ask ourselves a series of questions: How many shots are there? Why are there so many or so few? What is the purpose of each edit? Does it clarify the action? Does it excite the audience? Is it establishing a style? Is it creating suspense or adding emotion? Is the editing heavy-handed and manipulative, or is it more subtle, allowing us to draw our own conclusions? Is the editing a significant element in the film, or is it used as simply a means by which to tell the story?

Review

- Editing is the process of joining one piece of film to another.
- The two primary forms of editing are cutting to continuity and classical cutting.
- Pacing is the perceived speed of the action as it is manipulated by the number and frequency of edits.
- Montage is the process of connecting snippets of scenes together into a unified sequence (battle sequences, training sequences, etc.).

MOTION IN PICTURES

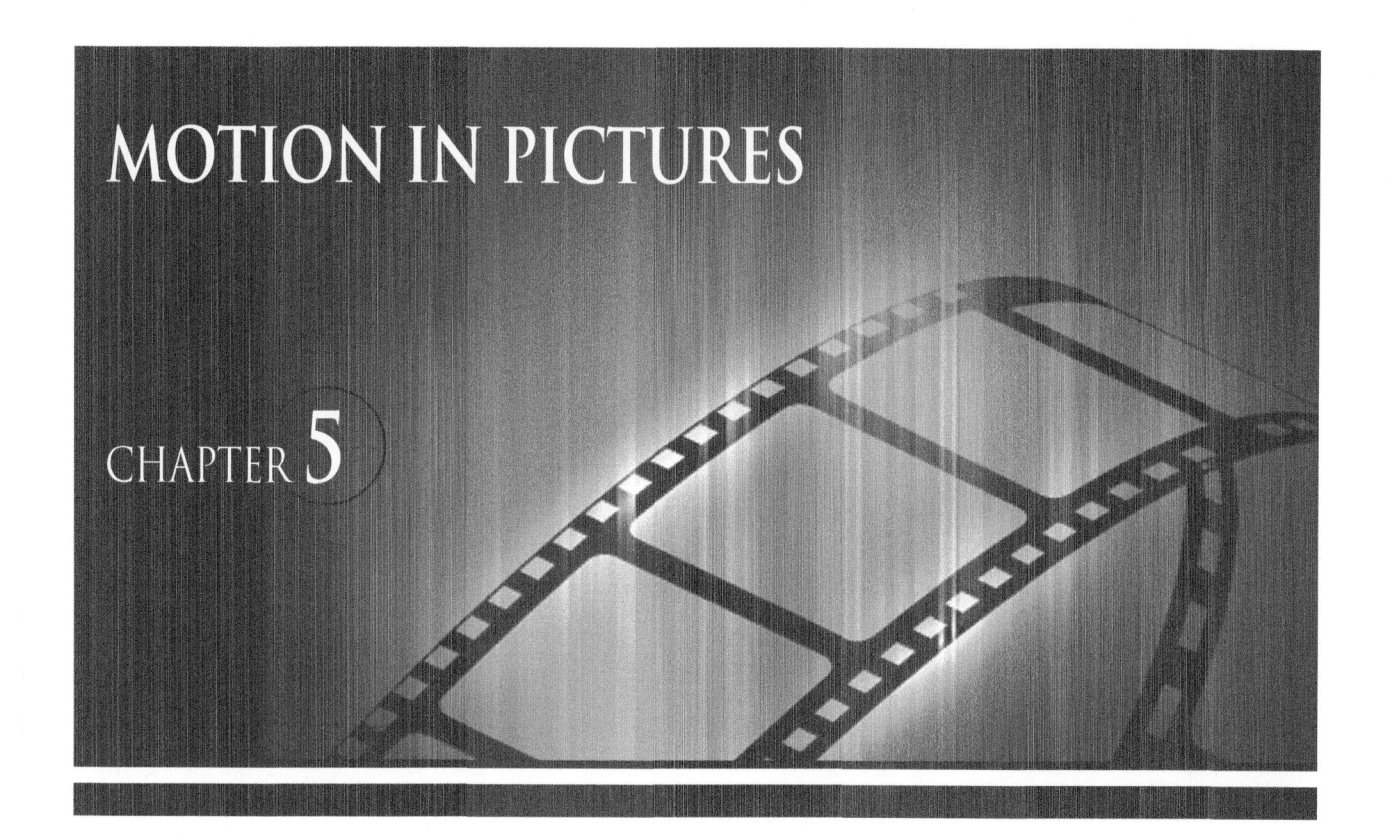

CHAPTER 5

The name "motion pictures" to describe film is a bit of a misnomer. What we are seeing on the screen is actually a series of still pictures shown in rapid succession, which our eyes perceive as motion. Despite that, it is still important to discuss how films use motion, or movement rather, to tell a story. There are three primary forms of movement in film: movement of the actor, movement of the camera, and movement of the film.

THE ACTOR

An actor can move for two reasons: for a practical reason or for an artistic reason. If an actor needs to move from the kitchen into the living room to get a coat, this is practical or concrete movement. Artistic movement, which is more **lyrical** and stylized, includes virtually any movement that is choreographed. **Choreographed** movement like dancing or fight scenes is movement that is designed to look a specific way by someone other than just the actor. The more lyrical and stylized the movement, the less realistic it is. Musicals often employ choreographed dance routines, and martial arts movies use very stylized fight sequences. Both films are using movement lyrically in an attempt to make the story more visually interesting and entertaining. Film is a visual medium; and stylized movement such as dance and martial arts definitely helps to make the visual elements more interesting to the audience.

In addition to the way actors move, the direction in which they move gives the audience important information. An actor can move left, right, up, down, diagonally, forward, and backward. Each of those movements tells a different story to the audience. Again, audiences don't react to this consciously but in the back of their minds, it makes an impact.

LEFT AND RIGHT

Film language was most fully developed in countries where reading is done left to right. As a result, movement from left to right across the screen feels normal and comfortable to the audience. If we see an actor moving left to right, we believe that things are going well or at least as they should be. Movement from right to left

The stylized movement and posing make for an exciting visual in Bob Fosse's Sweet Charity.

feels foreign and somewhat unnatural to us; therefore, actors moving in that direction make us feel as though something is wrong. We are concerned for their safety.

In the opening scene of *Raiders of the Lost Ark*, Indy is moving into the cave from left to right. We feel cautious but comfortable. When he takes the idol and everything begins falling apart (including a giant boulder rolling down to crush him), he moves from right to left. While we would still be worried for him because of falling debris and giant boulders, the movement against the grain adds to the feeling that things have gone wrong.

Movement side to side across the screen when the camera is stationary rather than simply moving in a specific direction with the camera following has a very different feel. This usually occurs in a long shot when we are far enough away for the actor or the action to move across the screen. This movement feels fast and exciting. It gives the audience the feeling that the action is so fast that we are unable to catch up to it.

UP AND DOWN

Movement up and down has nothing to do with how we read but, rather, what we associate with going up and going down. Movement upward signifies joy, success, inspiration. In real life we see people jumping for joy when they win or receive good news, and we feel the same way when we see actors on screen jumping or leaping in the air.

Downward movement has the opposite effect. We associate moving down with failure, depression, sadness and death. In the final scene of *Braveheart* (warning: spoiler alert), we see the small cloth that Wallace's wife made for him fall out of Wallace's hand. Though we don't see him die, this downward movement tells us all we need to know: He is dead.

FORWARD AND BACKWARD

Unlike any of the other forms of actor movement, how the audience feels about movement toward or away from the screen depends on how the audience feels about the character who is moving. If the character moving toward us is someone we have positive feelings toward—the hero, the young love interest, etc.—we feel positive about the movement. It feels safe, comforting, even intimate. If, however, the character moving toward us is a villain or a terrifying monster, we have very negative feelings about the movement. Movement toward the screen shows power and control, and movement away shows weakness and fear. This means if a hero is moving away, he has been defeated or turned away and we feel bad for him. If a villain is moving away, it means the same but the audience has a very different reaction—happy, inspired, vindicated.

Like movement across the camera, movement toward the camera from a long distance has a different connotation to audiences than the medium shots and full shots described earlier. Movement from a great distance toward the camera seems slow and interminable. In Monty Python's *The Holy Grail,* they play up this point in a scene where a knight is running toward a castle. They film him from a great distance, cut to the guards at the castle, and then back to the knight several times. Because they are mocking the point, they use the same shot of the knight each time so it not only seems to be taking forever, but he doesn't seem to be getting anywhere.

The further we are away from the action and the higher above it, the slower and more lyrical the movements seems. Conversely, the lower and closer we are to the action, the faster and more intense it appears.

The lack of motion can be used for two reasons: to show paralysis or complacency, and to give added power to any movement that does occur.

THE CAMERA

There are essentially seven ways in which a camera can move in a shot. Each method does something different to the action of the scene and has a different effect on the audience.

1. **Dolly**: This is a tracking shot. That means that it follows along with the movement in the scene. This can be accomplished by literally laying down tracks and placing the camera on a dolly, or it can be any shot moving alongside a moving vehicle. It allows the action of the scene to move forward while keeping us connected to it. A **pull-back dolly** shot is when the camera moves away from the action to reveal something that was not previously visible to the audience. This revelation is usually shocking or surprising. In *Gone With the Wind*, we see Scarlett tending to a few injured soldiers. When the camera pulls back, we see that there are in fact thousands of injured soldiers present. It surprises and overwhelms the audience with the magnitude of the carnage. While it is technically on a crane, the movement of the shot makes it a dolly shot.

42 Chapter 5

From a medium shot of a few soldiers and Scarlett, we pull-back to this image.

2. **Tilt:** In this shot, the camera looks up or down from a stationary point. This can be used a number of ways, yet it is most often a point-of-view shot that allows us to see the size or height of something. A man runs to the edge of a cliff and looks down; the camera shows what he sees looking out and then tilts down to show us the rocky coast several hundred feet below. Another example is a woman running around a corner. She suddenly stops and looks up, and we see a shot of a giant reptilian foot. The camera tilts up, showing us of the entire Godzilla standing just 20 feet away. It is similar to a pull-back dolly shot in that it usually reveals something to us that we hadn't seen before—something surprising or impressive.

3. **Pan:** In pan, the camera pivots from side to side while remaining stationary. A standard pan is slow and is used to keep side-to-side movement in frame. It can also show the physical relationship of two people or places. At the end of *The African Queen* (warning: spoiler alert), Humphrey Bogart and Katherine Hepburn find themselves trapped in high reeds, unable to finish their journey down the river. They are in bad condition and decide to give up, lie down, and die. If the director chooses to cut at this point and then shows us the place they are trying to reach, it only shows us that they failed. What the director does in this case is to pan past the reeds to show us that the place they are trying to reach is just beyond the reeds. They have made it. They don't have to give up. They don't have to die. It is a much more heart-breaking scene to use the pan rather than an edit.

A **swish-pan** is a very rapid pan across a space. It is so quick that the intermediary space is just a blur. It still suggests that the two subjects we are looking at are relatively close together, but it wipes out anything between them as unimportant. It also ups the excitement and pace of a scene.

4. **Crane:** In order to give the flexibility to go from a first person intimate relationship to the action to an omniscient, detached third person view or vice-versa rapidly directors will use a crane shot. The camera is attached to a large crane with a place for the camera man and director or cinematographer to sit. It can start at ground level and rise up and away or start high and come in close. A crane is often used in establishing shots, showing us where we are and then moving down and in to get a better look at the action of the scene.

5. **Aerial:** Taking a crane shot to far greater heights and distances is the aerial shot. Most often this shot is taken from a helicopter or plane. It allows the audience to see a large panorama of the action or location. It is almost always used as an establishing or re-establishing shot. It gives the audience the greatest feeling of detachment and can cover the greatest distance in all directions.

6. **Zoom:** Zoom is less a movement of the camera as it is a movement of the lens of a camera. Moving from a wide-angle lens to a telephoto lens or vice-versa will change the depth of field as well as the width of what the camera can see. A zoom allows the audience's view to go from further away to closer (or closer to further) without moving the camera.

7. **Hand-held:** A hand-held camera is exactly what it sounds like: The camera is held off the ground by the cameraman. It is smaller and more versatile, allowing the camera to get closer to the action. Depending on what the director wants, the camera can be stabilized so it is relatively smooth as it moves through the scene, or it can be held naturally to give a more chaotic and bouncy look. The *Bourne Identity* films are well known for their use of hand-held cameras in chase scenes. This makes the chase seem more frenetic, urgent and rough.

The advances in the technology of hand-held digital cameras has given directors even more flexibility and a greater opportunity to get the camera as close to the action as possible without losing quality.

THE FILM

Movement of the film is not a completely accurate description of the five remaining uses of movement in film, but it is close enough. Four of the examples are alterations in the speed or the manner in which the film is fed through the camera, and the other has to do with how the action is filmed.

1. **Slow motion:** Historically, film was projected at 16 frames per second. Today that speed is more likely to be 24 frames per second. The process of filming a scene to be shown in slow motion is that the rate at which it was filmed must be higher than the rate at which it is projected. The faster that it is filmed, the slower it will appear when shown in a theater. Modern technology now allows directors to film incredibly clear, incredibly slow sequences. In *Sherlock Holmes: Game of Shadows*, there is a sequence that was filmed at more than 1,000 frames per second. This allows us to see an incredibly fast-moving projectile and the damage it does clearly in frightening detail. What slow motion does is to make a rapidly moving sequence appear lyrical, poetic, and even solemn. It can take a violent shoot-out or fight and turn it in to something akin to ballet.

2. **Fast motion:** Fast motion is the opposite of slow motion in virtually every way. The process involves filming a scene at a slower rate than the rate at which it will be shown. Fast motion does not make anything seem lyrical or poetic; it makes it seem silly and comical. The British television show *Benny Hill* and the film *Tom Jones* both use fast motion for this purpose—to get a laugh and to make a scene that might seem fraught with danger seem safe.

3. **Freeze frame:** When the action on the screen does not appear to be changing at all, it is called a freeze frame. The audience perceives that the action has frozen in time. In reality, what has happened is that the same single frame has been reproduced hundreds of times to give the impression that there is no movement. The use of freeze frame adds significance to whatever image is being reproduced. The implication is that this moment is so important that the director wants to make sure

that you have time to see everything clearly and completely. It is often used to suggest death or a triumph over death, such as at the end of *Butch Cassidy and the Sundance Kid*.

4. **Reverse motion:** Like fast motion, reverse motion can try to make a heavy scene seem comic if it is reversed at a high enough speed to seem comical. Most often, though, reverse motion is used to show that we are traveling back in time. We see everything that we saw when the action of the scene was moving forward, but now we see it moving backward. What happens at this point is usually that the action begins again, almost certainly having a different outcome. The 1998 film *Sliding Doors* uses this premise quite effectively. Helen, a young woman who has just been fired from her job, is attempting to catch a subway to take her back home much earlier in the day than her deadbeat boyfriend is expecting her. We see her start down the stairs to the subway platform but she is redirected by a young girl playing with a doll heading up the stairs. As a result, Helen just misses the subway and the doors slide shut in front of her. Then the scene reverses to where Helen once again starts down the stairs. This time, the young girl's mother pulls her out of the way and Helen arrives at the subway before the doors close. The rest of the film explores how different her life turns out as a result of missing or catching the subway train.

5. **Animation:** Whereas the previous four examples looked at how the film was manipulated through the camera, animation has to do with how the subjects being filmed are manipulated. Animation includes cartoons, stop-action photography, and clay animation, often called Claymation. In each of the examples, the film is constructed one frame at a time. In cartoon animation a single shot is drawn

One of the more than 100,000 frames shot individually for Snow White and the Seven Dwarfs.

and photographed, then another, then another. In stop-action and Claymation, a scene is set up with still figures (dolls, clay figurines, etc.), then photographed. Again, this is done one single frame at a time. This means that a 90-minute film would require nearly 130,000 set-ups and photographs. Improvements in technology have altered the way cartoon animation is done. It can now be done digitally at a much quicker pace. It still requires many small adjustments, but it is nowhere nearly as time-consuming as it was in the past.

In analyzing the motion in a movie, we should remember that every one of the ways discussed above is a conscious specific decision made by the directors, choreographers, and cinematographers. Each choice tells the audience something important about the story, the characters, and the events of the film.

Review

- Movement in film can be concrete or lyrical.
- There are three sources of movement in film: the actor, the camera, and the film.
- Actors' movement up and down, left to right, and forward and backward each have different effects on the audience.
- The camera can move a number of ways: side to side with either a dolly shot or a pan, up and down with a tilt shot, in or out with a crane shot or zoom, overhead with an aerial shot, or in a shakier more immediate way with a hand-held shot.
- Film can be slowed down, sped up, frozen, or reversed; each for a very different effect. It can be moved forward a frame at a time to make still objects seem alive in animation.

COLLABORATION: DIRECTION AND DESIGN

CHAPTER 6

The old joke goes, To err is human, but to really mess things up requires a committee." The premise is that the more people you have in the decision-making process, the worse the final result. This is why filmmaking, while it is a tremendously collaborative enterprise, leaves the final decisions to the director, at least for the first cut. Making a movie requires collaboration, but not in the same way as a committee would. Dozens, sometimes hundreds of people work on a movie, but they are all working toward one goal: achieving the director's vision. Smart directors will surround themselves with talented people and give them the opportunity to do what they do best. Smart directors will offer feedback and provide guidance. In this chapter we will explore what directors do and how they bring all of those hundreds of individuals together.

STAGE VS. SCREEN

The position of the director was first recognized as a separate function many of hundreds of years before the first film was made. It was created for the production of plays, and it set fairly clearly the function of directors. They would act as a proxy for the audience during rehearsals and provide the overriding vision of the show. While this is a good starting point, it is important to understand the differences between stage plays and movies and how those differences affect what a director must do.

Film is a visual medium, while theater is a verbal medium. The technical side of most plays involves costumes, lighting, and scenic design, but the limitation of the theater and what can be accomplished live make those decisions less complicated and less significant. Some of the most important decisions in starting work on a film have to do with where to shoot the scenes—on-location versus a sound stage or studio lot. A stage director has no such decision. The play will be performed in a specific theater with a specific size and shape; even shows that travel don't usually have theaters that vary greatly in size and shape of the performance space.

Another set of decisions that are unique to film involve shot selection. On stage, the audience member is the same distance away and has the same point-of-view of the action throughout the play. The film director can and must change the audience's point-of-view. It is a major aspect of the filmmaker's art.

A film director can do something a stage director really can't, which is to manipulate time. We discussed in the previous chapter that film allows us to use fast motion, slow motion, reverse motion, and freeze frame. Film can also use montage and editing to compress the amount of time it takes for something to occur. In a play, time can, with a few rare exceptions, move faster or slower than real time only in between scenes. A scene on stage that takes 3 minutes to watch generally covers 3 minutes of action. A film can, in those same 3 minutes, cover 10 seconds or 10 weeks.

This is not to say that a film director's job is more difficult or less difficult than that of a stage director. They are simply quite different. Stage is an actor's medium. Once a play starts, regardless of what the director may want to happen, the actor is actually performing the show and can and does, to some extent, alter what the director's vision was every single night. Film is a director's medium. Directors can re-shoot a scene over and over until it looks precisely the way they want it to look.

DIRECTOR'S VISION

We have talked previously about director's vision. Let's take some time now to look at how that vision is achieved. The primary influence on how completely the director's vision will appear in the final cut is the producer. The producer and, by extension, the production company make the two decisions that most affect what a director can accomplish: setting the budget, and final cut. We have talked before about final cut—the ability to decide what version of the completed film will appear in theaters. Directors with final cut have much greater control than those without it over achieving their vision. The budget has an even more profound effect on what the film will ultimately look like. Directors may have many wonderful ideas for the movies they are making, but if the budget of the film is $2 million versus $100 million, that is going to change everything.

We mentioned earlier that "smart directors" will let those around them do their jobs and provide guidance and feedback. This is the essence of collaboration. There are, however, directors who are not as comfortable with collaboration and want to do as much of the film themselves as they possibly can. This type of director, called an **auteur director**, does not want to make just the final decision but instead wants to be intimately involved throughout the process. Sometimes this results in a very good film, and sometimes not so much. For directors who want to involve their collaborators more, the process of putting together a film would look something like the following.

COSTUME DESIGN

In designing the costumes, which includes hairstyle, make-up and accessories, there are a number of decisions that the director and costumer make together about each character:

1. **Era:** The first decision is the time period in which the action takes place. Is the costume accurate for the period or not? If it isn't, why isn't it? A science fiction film in which someone travels back in time might justify wearing clothes that are not true to the time period. Otherwise, the costumes should reflect the era and send a message that lets the audience know when the film is taking place.

2. **Social status:** What is the income and social class of the characters? If they are members of high society, their clothes would be of a finer quality than if they were homeless or impoverished. Again, we can use costume to go against their status if they are trying to hide their wealth or poverty.

3. **Gender:** Depending on the era, women and men may have wildly different ways of dressing. While today men and women can both wear t-shirts and jeans, in the 1800s the genders wore clothing that clearly identified whether they were male or female. Gender-specific clothing can be used against form if a character is trying to pass as a member of the opposite sex, a common trick in Shakespeare's comedies.

4. **Age:** The age of the characters might also affect the type and style of clothing they wear. Generally speaking, the older characters are, the more conservatively they dress. The question of age is twofold: How old are they, and how age-appropriate is their clothing? For example, you may have a woman who is in her 40s but wants everyone to believe that she is in her 20s. The result might be a costume that is not appropriate for a 40-year-old woman, telling the audience a great deal about the character.

5. **Silhouette:** The outline of the characters' clothing can tell the audience a good deal about them as well. A young girl in an over-sized jacket and sweatpants is very different from one wearing skin-tight jeans and top. In the Civil War era the impracticality of the large hoop dresses illustrates that greater emphasis was being placed on appearance than on functionality.

6. **Texture:** Each style of fabric has a different feel and conveys something different about the character who wears them. Do we feel the same toward a character who wears a silk shirt as one who wears a flannel shirt? Do jeans evoke the same feelings as corduroys or leather pants? What kind of person would wear a flannel shirt and jeans? A lumberjack? Who else? What kind of person would wear leather pants and a silk shirt?

7. **Color:** We discussed earlier how color can affect an audience. In terms of costuming, clothing can suggest mood, style, or an affiliation. In virtually every production of *Romeo & Juliet*, the two feuding families, the Montagues and Capulets, are presented wearing opposing color schemes. In the 1968 version the Capulets wore red and yellow while the Montagues wore blue and gray. Color can also suggest a lack of affiliation. In the photo below from *Hamlet*, we see that everyone else is dressed in bright colors—yellows, reds, ivory—while Hamlet is dressed entirely in black. It shows immediately that he has set himself apart from the "crowd" and that he is in mourning.

One of these things is not like the others.

8. **Practicality:** Above, we briefly discussed the Civil War era hoop skirts and how impractical they were. The next element of a costume to consider is its practicality or purpose. Does it have a specific purpose? Is it a uniform? Is it sleepwear? Is it beachwear? I remember a student turning in a costume design that had a young woman wearing a business suit complete with briefcase, for going to work, which seems plausible enough. Unfortunately, the character worked as a lifeguard at the YWCA, so a business suit would have been so unacceptable for that purpose as to have been a firing offense. While the previous example is an obvious mistake, you can have a film with a character who wears an outfit that is ill-suited for the task at hand. It shows that the director and costumer don't understand the task or that they are out of touch.

9. **Body exposure:** How much skin is visible in the costume? A woman dressed in a long dress with a high collar and opera gloves conveys that she is formal, conservative, and demure. The same woman dressed in a halter top and short shorts would convey an entirely different image; the more skin showing, the more provocative the outfit.

10. **Accessories:** In addition to clothing, what kind of earrings, glasses, necklaces, watches, and other accessories is the character wearing? Each of those choices needs to echo what the other elements have established. Conservative clothing will almost always be matched with conservative accessories. Expensive clothing is matched with expensive accessories, and so on.

While make-up and hair aren't technically accessories, they are elements that don't have the same properties that clothing does. Make-up in film is used to a far less degree than on stage. In live theater all actors wear make-up, whether their character would or not, in order to be seen more clearly by the audience. In film the camera can and does get closer to the actor so the features do not need to be accentuated by make-up the way they do on stage. In the movies, make-up is often used as a special effect or to show some level of artifice on behalf of the characters; they are trying to hide something or to change themselves for some reason. In *Batman: The Dark Knight* the make-up of the Joker tells us much about his character: He is different, he is altering his appearance to create an alter-ego, and the disheveled appearance adds to the sense of his chaotic nature.

All of these elements combine to establish the overall image for each character in the film. Every one of the decisions above is taken into consideration for each character in the film. The extent to which attention is paid to the smallest details is affected by how significant the character is in the film. Extras (we will talk about them in a later chapter) often bring their own clothing if the film takes place in or around present-day.

Smeared, cracked, and all over the place, the Joker's make-up illustrates his inner turmoil.

Now that we see what the decisions are, let's talk briefly about how the decisions are made. A director will meet with the costume designer prior to work beginning on the movie. They will discuss overall themes, era, styles, and the like. The director will go through most of the featured characters and make any comments about their vision for each role. The director may say something as vague as, "She's happy and demure, bright colors, conservative outfits." Or be a little more specific: "He's a bit of a hippy, loose-fitting clothes, dirty, old, layered, maybe some cool retro-looking stuff." After the meeting, the costumer will go back and draw sketches for each character discussed and bring back the sketches in color, usually with a swatch of fabric planned to use for each piece. The director will look at the sketches and give feedback. What the director likes will move forward into production. The other items will be altered and brought back for more feedback and final directorial approval.

SCENIC DESIGN

Scenic design deals with the surroundings in every shot. It includes landscape, buildings, sky, even weather. The director and the scenic designer work together on a number of decisions concerning the settings and surrounding decor.

1. **Indoor or outdoor:** This first decision is dictated almost entirely by the script, though it will be affected by other decisions. Does the scene take place indoors or outdoors? If it specifies one or another, how important is it that the action takes place there? Does the scene have to be outdoors, or does it make more sense to move it indoors? How does the setting interact with the characters? Is it simply the backdrop for the action, or is it part of the action? Outdoor filming has a drawback in that weather and other uncontrollable variables increase the level of difficulty. However, if the scene is about getting chased through a cornfield, you can't really film it inside.

2. **Location:** Where should the movie be filmed in its entirety? There are advantages to filming on location, and there are also advantages to filming at the studio. Location gives the movie a more authentic feel. If the movie takes place in Ireland and you are actually filming in Ireland, that will show in the final cut. The major drawbacks to filming on location are time and money. If the decision is made to film on location, location scouts are sent out to find a place suitable for the movie. Once they find a locale that meets the director's vision, they must determine how much it is going to cost to film there. Costs include paying the owners of the land, the town in which you are filming, getting all of the supplies, technicians, and actors to the locale, finding all of them places to stay while they are on location, and more. The film *State and Main* shows this process well in a very entertaining way. The advantages of shooting on a studio lot or soundstage are exactly what the disadvantages to shooting on location are: time and money. The cost of filming at the studio is significantly less, and there is no waiting around to find the location, get permits to shoot, get a schedule approved, etc. It is safe to imagine that most directors would prefer to shoot on location and get their vision perfectly, but that is not always a possibility. Budget restrictions can force directors to make concessions, as can time constraints and the inability to find exactly the location for which they are looking.

3. **Style:** What is the overall style of the location? This has to do with the style of the film first. If the movie is trying to be more realistic, the setting should reflect that style. If it is trying to be more formalistic, that should be reflected in the scenic elements. The science fiction film *Alien* had a very specific style in the lighting and the shape and design of the ship Nostromo. It echoed the style of the film as a whole. The second way that style appears in scenic design is in the style of the particular location. If the film takes place in the 1930s, the location will likely include art deco elements. If the scene is in a person's house, the style should reflect that character's specific style.

4. **Era:** As with costuming, when the film takes place has a profound effect on the design. It would seem that the time in which the film takes place would dictate the era of the setting, but that is not always the case. If the film is set today but the house in which it takes place is a "creepy colonial mansion," the setting would need to reflect the time period in which the mansion was built, not today.

5. **Social Status:** Social status, in terms of setting, has to do with the status of the owner of the location. A poor neighborhood would have a low social status and should be visibly represented in the scenic design regardless of whether or not the characters in the scene are poor.

6. **Size:** The size of the scenery tells the audience something about the film. The larger the things are, the more power, wealth and pride are associated with them. In the film *Jurassic Park* the park's owner repeatedly says, "No expense was spared," so the park should look like it. The gates leading into the park are giant wooden doors; it looks as though no expense was spared.

7. **Furnishings:** How is the scene decorated? Previous elements such as social status, style, and era will affect decorations up to a point. Additional considerations have to do with how densely decorated the scene is, how neatly decorated it is, and more. In *Glory*, Matthew Broderick's character Colonel Shaw confronts Colonel Montgomery about his illegal dealings in pillaging Southern homes and sending the spoils back to his family to be used for profit. He is in Montgomery's makeshift "office," and the room is filled to overflowing with expensive decorations: silver candle holders, gold boxes, and much, much more. The setting illustrates Montgomery's guilt clearly and completely.

8. **Atmosphere:** The overall feel of the setting is the combination of the other elements discussed. If the scene is taking place in a happy children's playhouse, all the elements should work to create the appropriate atmosphere. Atmosphere reflects the style of the film, its concept, and the tone of the specific scene.

Much in the same way that the director interacts with the costumer, the director and scenic designer meet to discuss scenes in broad terms. Designers work up sketches and floor plans, bring them back to the director for feedback, then re-works the design until they feel that they have achieved the director's vision.

If the director decides to film on location, the producers will put together a team of location scouts. The scouts will meet with the director to determine precisely what is required for each location. The scouts then go out and look for places that most closely re-create the director's vision. Once locations are found, schedules, contracts, and travel arrangements are made. The needs of a location can be something as vague as a "small New England town" or far more specific. The key element of the location can be an old mill or a scenic background. Film companies have been known to find a piece of land, buy or rent it, and then build whatever settings they need on location. Once the film company leaves, the settings may be left as is or torn down.

When George Lucas decided to make a new *Star Wars* film after 16 years, he was happy to be able to return to the same location in Tunisia where sets had been created for the planet Tatooine. The set remained almost perfectly intact, and they were able to start shooting almost immediately. The same was true for Peter Jackson when he started filming *The Hobbit* nearly a decade after concluding the last *Lord of the Rings* movie.

Review

Take a scene from a movie that you have watched in class and analyze the 10) elements of costume design (describe and discuss what it tells the audience about the characters and the scene).

Era

Social Status

Gender

Age

Silhouette

Texture

Color

Practicality

Body Exposure

Accessories

Take the same scene from above and analyze the 8 elements of scenic design (describe and discuss what it tells the audience about the characters and the scene).

Indoor/Outdoor

Location

Style

Era

Social Status

Chapter 6

Size

Furnishings

Atmosphere

SCREENPLAY

CHAPTER 7

The screenplay is the written representation of the film; it is where the film is born. The place where the screenplay is born is inside the mind of the screen writer. The story of the film, often called the **narrative**, is part structure, part storytelling technique, part **genre**, and part style. In this chapter we are going to look at structure and technique. We will explore the process whereby an idea becomes a screenplay and a screenplay becomes a film.

STRUCTURE

There are a number of ways that writers can choose to structure their screenplay. We will look at some of the most common forms.

CLIMACTIC STRUCTURE

The oldest and simplest way to put together a story is climactic structure. In this format we begin with a hero (protagonist) and villain (antagonist). The first step in the storytelling is called exposition. **Exposition** is where the writer introduces us to the characters and the world of the film. It gives the audience a view of the world in **stasis**. The world of the film is moving forward just as it has been until something happens to change that. The exposition gives us a clear image of what the world in stasis looks like.

A well-written exposition reveals this information to the audience naturally in a way that seems realistic and reasonable. The exception, of course, is if the style of the film is formalistic, in which case the information should reflect the style of the film. Poorly written exposition jams awkward sentences into characters' mouths to get the information out: "Good morning, Tom. I, your long-lost brother Jim, with whom you have just recently been reunited, have made you breakfast." If the world of the film is too foreign to the audience, it may be necessary to insert some narration or information on the screen. Science fiction or fantasy films like *Star Wars* and *Lord of the Rings* have a great deal of complicated information to give the audience that could not be reasonably conveyed to the audience through natural dialogue.

Once the exposition has established the world of the film, the action of the story begins to unfold: The hero has some great goal, and the villain, who may be a person, a group of people, or society itself, stands in the way. The story evolves through a series of scenes that move the characters toward a climactic moment: a battle, an argument, a decision, etc. This is called the **rising action**. The rising action takes up almost the entire time of the story. It is most often a series of cause-and-effect situations that move the story forward. Once we reach the **climax**, the hero wins or loses the battle, wins or loses the girl or whatever the specifics of the story may be. We then begin the resolution or **falling action** that takes us to the end of the story and a new stasis: the world as it will be going forward. Whether it be "happily ever after" or a "sadder but wiser" world, the action has stabilized to a new normal from which the future will unwind.

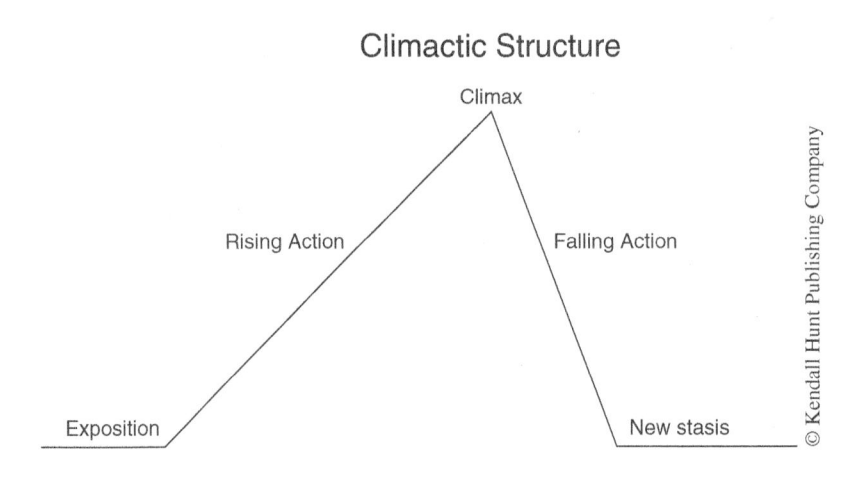

Climactic Structure

[Diagram showing a triangular plot structure with Exposition at bottom left, Rising Action going up, Climax at top, Falling Action going down, and New stasis at bottom right]

© Kendall Hunt Publishing Company

THREE-ACT STRUCTURE

The most common story structure for film is the three-act structure. This is a form of the climactic structure with a few key alterations. The first act takes up about 25% of the length of the film. It includes the exposition followed by the initial **trigger event**, that is, the event that disrupts the world in stasis and the first major plot point: the **point of no return**. This is where the hero makes a decision that forces movement forward. There is no longer a chance to go back to the original world in stasis from the exposition.

The second act covers the middle 50% of the film. In this act the plot is moving steadily towards the climax. Somewhere in the second half of the second act, the second major plot point occurs: the **reversal**. This moment is a major setback for the hero or heroes, it is the point where it looks as though they will not reach their goal; they will not succeed. The reversal often sends the action spinning off in a different and unexpected direction.

The third act encompasses the final 25% of the film and includes the climax, the falling action, and the new stasis. The climax is the most important part of the film; therefore, it is the third act that is the most important act. If a movie is going to fall apart, it will usually do so either early in the first act or in the third act.

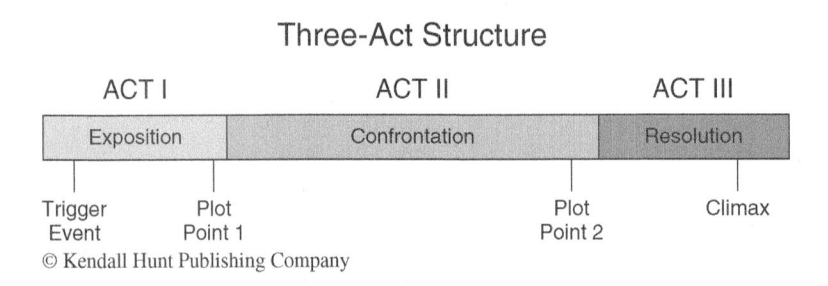

Three-Act Structure

ACT I	ACT II	ACT III
Exposition	Confrontation	Resolution

Trigger Event — Plot Point 1 — Plot Point 2 — Climax

© Kendall Hunt Publishing Company

In the film *Hancock*, the story is moving forward fine until the final act. In the first half of the movie, Hancock himself is virtually indestructible. When we reach the reversal, we discover that another person has similar powers and, despite the two having been in the same city for some time, we come to find that if they are too close to one another, both will lose their powers. As a result, in the third act Hancock is in a much weakened state due to his proximity to Mary, the other super being. As fate would have it, at this exact moment, the chief villain, who has no reason to suspect that Hancock is weak, decides to attack him. This is weak writing, a plot hole. If the villain doesn't know Hancock is not himself, why would he attack him? Surely he must expect to get trounced the way he did early in the film.

A well written screenplay will have strong, logical plot points that make sense. Another third act problem is the "surprise ending," where we discover something that we never suspected. Again, if it is well-written, the surprise ending makes sense and, upon looking back at the film, we can see that the clues were there; we just weren't paying close enough attention. *The Sixth Sense* is a terrific example. Once you know what the surprise is, you can go back and watch the film again and see that it all adds up. A poorly written third act surprise will come out of nowhere and not hold up upon re-examination of the film.

CIRCULAR STRUCTURE

The third most common way to build the story is called a circular structure. In this format the movie starts near the end of story, usually just prior to the climax. Then it flashes back to the beginning of the story. From here it moves much in the same way that your typical three-act story would until it rejoins the opening moment. It then continues on through the climax, falling action, and new stasis. This method is often used to catch audiences' attention right at the start and pull them in before establishing the original world in stasis and the exposition. If not a purely attention-getting technique, a circular structure can be used to create a level of mystery. The 2006 film *Inside Man* begins with actor Clive Owen stuck in a very small space. We don't know where he is, or why he is there. As the story unfolds, the audience is left wondering how he will end up stuck inside that small space and why.

There are other ways to structure a film, particularly the more formalistic the style of the film. Story structure gives the screen writer a format to use, a skeleton upon which to build the story. However, as we have seen above, structure is not enough; the story must still be well-written. Now let's take a look at the process of writing a screenplay.

PROCESS

The process of writing is much more difficult than it sounds. Author Gene Fowler once said, "Writing is easy: All you do is sit staring at a blank sheet of paper until drops of blood form on your forehead." A writer must first have an idea. Ideas can come from a number of sources: other written works, dreams, real-life experiences, history, myths, something overheard, even hallucinations. An idea that comes from a previously written work is called an **adapted screenplay**. This can be a film based on a book, a poem, a song, a play or even a previously made film. An **original screenplay** is one for which the idea comes entirely from the writers themselves. Once they have an idea, they can begin the writing process

WHAT IS DIFFERENT ABOUT TODAY?

The first and most important question that must be answered by writers is, "What is different about today?" The world of their story is in stasis; things are moving along the way they always have. At this point we are waiting for the trigger event, the action that upsets the stasis and moves the story forward. Writer who don't know what is different about today have no starting point for their story. It is important to begin the action just prior to the first trigger event. If the action starts too early, the audience grows bored and loses interest; too late and the audience doesn't understand what is going on.

In *One Flew Over the Cuckoo's Nest*, McMurphy is about to be committed to an insane asylum. The action starts with McMurphy making the choice to go to the asylum instead of prison. McMurphy entering the asylum is the trigger event. It will forever alter his world and the world of the other inmates in the asylum. If we start the action of the film earlier, it will take too long to get the "real action" of the story going. If we start later, we miss the trigger and we don't have a clear idea of what the world in stasis was like before the initial trigger.

The opening event is called a trigger because, much like firing a gun, it is a significant event that sets action in motion. The trigger causes something else to happen this new event becomes the next trigger which causes something else, which becomes the next trigger and so on. This is how the writer builds the plot and moves the story forward—trigger and action, trigger and action.

Genre

Once the writer has an idea and a trigger event, the next decision involves the style and genre of the film. This may not be a conscious decision. It may develop naturally out of the idea. Some ideas might naturally become a romantic comedy or horror film, etc. **Genre** is a category or sub-category of film: action, romance, horror, science fiction, Western, documentary, drama, martial arts, film noir, and many more. The most general genres are comedy and tragedy. Comedies end happily, while tragedies end sadly. Both genres have their basis in pain; it is merely in the outcomes where they differ. For example, in both a comedy and a tragedy, we may have a character that falls down the stairs. What is different is what happens next. In a comedy, characters get up, embarrassed and disheveled but uninjured, and go on with whatever they were doing. In a tragedy, the characters might be badly injured, paralyzed, or even killed in the fall.

Each genre has its own set of rules and outcomes that is followed in plot and structure. Perhaps the easiest to explain are the rules of the romantic comedy: boy meets girl, boy loses girl, boy gets girl. There are more rules and more specific elements, but that is the basic format of virtually every romantic comedy ever written.

In the earliest days of film, all movies belonged to one genre: documentary. They were attempting to document an event, nothing more, nothing less. Even though this was the first genre, filmmakers were not conscious that they were creating a genre. They were merely trying to use this new technology in the best way they knew how. Over the years, new genres developed. Some grew out of old genres and some were created on their own, but each genre went through the same cycle as it developed.

Genre Cycle

The genre cycle is a four-stage process through which each genre develops. The first stage of the cycle is the **primitive stage**. In this stage filmmakers may not, at first, even be aware that they are creating a new genre. The rules and format for the genre are still unclear. Through trial and error the new genre develops its form and conventions. This stage can have a significant impact on the audience because of the novelty of the genre. It is new and unlike what audiences have seen and are expecting.

Once the genre has established its rules, structure, and conventions completely, it has entered the second stage of development: the **classical stage**. Most films in any genre will be part of the classical stage of development. Once a genre has reached this stage, no new film in the genre can be said to be primitive. The rules are set, so there is no going back. The audience now knows what to expect and looks forward to getting it.

Some people find something they like and they stick with it, and others always want something new and novel. Filmmakers are no different. While most films in a genre will fit comfortably into the mold of the classical stage, some grow bored of the "same old thing" and want to try something new. Those who do try to break out of the rules and conventions of a genre often push it into its third phase: the **revisionist stage**. These films push or even fight against the rules of the genre. Western films, for example, had for years established clear good guys and bad guys with damsels in distress needing to be saved. When the films moved into the revisionist stage, the characters became more complex: Good guys weren't purely good, women became stronger, and the action wasn't so clearly black and white. Revisionist films are more complex and intellectual. They challenge the audience's expectations, asking them to look at the genre in a different way.

At this point in the development of the genre, some filmmakers may have grown tired of all the rules and choose not to challenge them as they would in a revisionist film but, rather, to mock them. When the rules and expectations of the genre are being made fun of, we have reached the **parody stage**. It is important to remember with parodies that they are making fun of the established elements of a specific genre. Do not assume that any comic film is a parody; it may simply be a comedy. Comedy is the genre least likely to be parodied because it is hard to make fun of a genre whose chief rules are making fun of something else.

Mel Brooks' Western parody Blazing Saddles includes the sexy, sultry singer and then adds dancing nineteenth-century German soldiers for a touch of the ridiculous.

To help clarify the stages further, let us take a look at the Western genre in general and some specific film examples that illustrate each stage of its development.

Primitive: Many Westerns from the early 1900s can fit this stage. One of the most famous examples is the 1903 film *The Great Train Robbery*. It may be the first Western ever made, and it was used as a template for Westerns for years to come.

Classical: Director John Ford is known as one of the greatest filmmakers in the genre. His 1939 film *Stagecoach* is still regarded as one of the all-time best Westerns. By this time, the rules that were first introduced in *The Great Train Robbery* had been codified and solidified into a standard format for the genre. From this point forward (and probably for several years before, no Western film can be considered primitive. The rules are set, so there is no going back.

Revisionist: Westerns already began to fight against the standard format by the early 1950s, and by the end of the 1960s, many films of the genre were in outright revolt: 1969's *The Wild Bunch* questioned the rules of a clear good-versus-evil battle. It challenged many of the ideas that were embraced in the original Westerns.

Parody: Mel Brooks has made a career out of taking different genres and mocking them mercilessly. His 1973 film *Blazing Saddles* is a pitch-perfect parody of the Western genre. It mocks the good-versus-evil premise. It points out the inherent racism in many of the early Westerns and, perhaps most important, it comments on the rules ironically.

Today we can still find Westerns that are classical, such as the 2007 re-make of the *3:10 to Yuma* and the 2006 *Broken Trail*. Or they may be revisionist, which may be the most popular version of Westerns today, like *Brokeback Mountain* and Baz Luhrman's *Australia*. Or parody, like *Shanghai Noon*.

Each genre and sub-genre will go through this cycle, some much more quickly than others. Sometimes what may start out as a revisionist version of one genre may develop into its own genre. If we look at the horror genre, we can see where it has split into many sub-genres: monster movies, teen slasher films, torture films, haunted house films, ghost movies, and many, many more.

FILM NOIR

There is one genre that has had a very unusual trip through the genre cycle. It is unique enough to warrant a brief discussion of its own. Film noir—which is French for black film—is a stylish and very dark style of film. It is most often associated with the shadowy detective stories that were so popular in Hollywood from the early 1930s until the late 1940s. Film noir embraced a visual style that was different from what was going on at the time, making extensive use of low-key lighting and unbalanced composition. The standard format of the genre has a man who is either a hard-boiled detective or a cop or an ordinary guy. Whichever the case, he has some moral code and generally wants to do what is right. As the story develops, he gets trapped by a femme fatale, a dangerous and beautiful woman who convinces him to do something wrong, usually murder. There is some debate over what the "classic" ending to a film noir should be. Most of the films end badly with the characters either dead or arrested, but many have an ambivalent ending and a few even have an ending where at least one character escapes punishment. The overall feel of the film, however, is dark and bleak.

After the end of the 1940s, the popularity of film noir dropped considerably. The 1950's decade, was, on the whole, more optimistic, and the dark, cynical view espoused in film noir no longer held sway with the audiences. There are a few films that some critics choose to classify as noir from the decade, but far fewer than in the previous 20 years.

The 1960s, and to a greater extent the 1970s, saw a minor increase in the number and quality of noir films. From 1962's *Cape Fear* to 1974's *Chinatown*, the genre continued to survive, if not exactly thrive. In the 1980s and 1990s, we began seeing a new kind of film noir that was far more erotically charged than its predecessor. Films like *Body Heat*, *Black Widow*, *Poison Ivy*, and *Basic Instinct* revitalized the genre with new energy and sexuality. This neo-noir was not as well received critically, though it did find commercial success, particularly in the burgeoning VCR and DVD markets.

We still see the classic noir-style films today with movies like *Sin City*, *A History of Violence*, *Mulholland Drive*, and *Insomnia*. Another offshoot of film noir is the sci-fi noir. These films have a structure similar to the classical noir but have changed the location from the seedy urban sprawl of the 30s and 40s to a futuristic society, often on another planet. Films like *Blade Runner* and *Dark City* embrace the dark world view of noir but, by placing the situation in an often wildly different environment, they can hide or alter the effect that the theme has on the film as a whole.

The 2005 neo-noir Sin City employs the black-and-white film, the stark contrasting shadows and light, then ups the stakes with flashes of color in the background.

Like most other genres, film noir also falls prey to the biting satire of the parody. Perhaps the earliest parody of the genre was Bob Hope's *My Favorite Brunette*, which debuted all the way back in 1947. Other more recent parodies include Neil Simon's *The Cheap Detective* (1978) and Steve Martin's *Dead Men Don't Wear Plaid* (1982) featuring Christopher Walken in a big dance number.

Film noir is the most under-recognized genre in film. This is due to the fact that most audiences don't realize that the genre even exists and the ones that do often argue over what constitutes a true film noir.

CONFLICT

Once screen writers have a clear idea of what the basic story idea is, what the first trigger is, and what the genre or at least the tone of the film is, they can begin writing the screen play. The process of actually putting words on paper (or computer screen) is a difficult one. It is important for the writer to build the story with strong and logical plot points while also developing the characters. The key to all stories in film is conflict. Drama is conflict. In the same way that no one would want to watch a football game with only one team playing, no one wants to see a film where there is no conflict.

How is conflict created? Each story has a hero or protagonist, who has some goal. The conflict arises when someone or something stands in the way of the hero achieving that goal. The barrier could be society (*Schindler's List*), family (*Romeo & Juliet*), an arch enemy (*The Dark Knight*), or some flaw in the heroes themselves (*Raging Bull*). As the plot develops, the barrier becomes stronger and more formidable, making the conflict greater until the climax of the story, where the hero is finally forced to face whatever that opposing force is and to defeat it or be defeated by it.

PRODUCTION

Once the screenplay has been written and re-written and re-written and so on and writers have what they believe to be a finished product, they must move on to getting the film produced. Less than 5% of all screenplays are ever produced. That number has been growing in recent years with access to online sources like YouTube, but it is still a very small percentage. If the screenplay is going to be made into a film, there are two directions writers can take: They can produce the film themselves, or they can seek out an agent who will work to get the film made by a professional production company.

Self-producing the film is getting easier and less expensive all the time. With the price of modern digital cameras and digital editing software, a film can be made for perhaps a tenth of what it cost 20 years ago. Once the film is made, it can be sent to production companies, posted to the Internet, or entered into one of the various film festivals around the world. If the film is successful in one of those venues, it can be purchased by a studio that will then distribute the film on a larger scale. Depending on what the studio perceives the value and potential of the film to be, it can pay as much as $5 million or as little as $2,000.

Finding an agent can be a difficult process. Once writers have an agent and have established themselves as legitimate screen writers, the process of getting a screenplay produced is much shorter and much easier. Unknown writers, though, face a much more daunting journey. Most agents do not accept unsolicited manuscripts. The ones who do have readers—people whose sole job is to read manuscripts and decide if the manuscript is worth passing on to an agent for consideration. If a manuscript makes it to an agent who decides it is worthy of representation, it gets passed on to readers at different studios in and around Hollywood. Again, those readers will decide if the screenplay is worth being sent on to their bosses for consideration. If it gets passed on to a producer and the producer likes the script, the producer will begin negotiations with the agent.

There are two ways that a studio can gain the rights to a screenplay: They can option it or buy it outright. If a studio options the film, it purchases the sole rights to make the film for a period of time. Most options are six months to one year. During that time, no one else is allowed to make the film. At any time during the option, the studio can decide to make the film, at which time it would pay an additional amount of money to purchase the rights completely. If it decides not to make the film at the end of the option time, the rights for the screenplay return to the writer, who can then shop the film around to other studios to see if one of those companies want to produce it. The writer keeps the money that the studio paid for the option rights.

Regardless of which route the screenplay takes, from writing to production, once a studio purchases the film, it owns the film. It is no different than selling a house or a car. The studio can now do with the script whatever they want to do. They can make the film, re-write the film, or use the pages to wallpaper their bathroom. It belongs to them now. As always, there are exceptions to the rule. If a writer is well established or the screenplay is in high demand, the studio is more willing to give away some of that power in order to get the much sought-after script. For example, the *Harry Potter* series was so highly valued that the original writer, J. K. Rowling, was given the power to approve actors, directors, and story changes. This is a rare case, and most writers have little recourse once they have sold the screenplay to the studio.

The credits of a film sometimes will list two or three writers. This does not mean that they all sat down together to work on the screenplay at the same time. What it usually means is that one writer wrote the original version of the film and that another was brought in to re-write a section or add more scenes, and so on. Once writers sell the film, the only power they have is to demand that their names be taken off the film if they feel it has been altered too much from their original vision. The fact is that many films are changed during shooting and in the editing process. Actors may make demands or find something that works better; a director can decide that a scene isn't working and change it; a producer may find that there is not enough in the budget to include a particular sequence.

For example, in *Raiders of the Lost Ark* there is a famous scene where a large bad guy with a scimitar is menacing Indiana Jones, but rather than fighting him, Jones takes out his gun and shoots him. It is a funny and memorable moment, but it was not written that way. During the filming, actor Harrison Ford became quite ill. On the day that the scene in question was scheduled, Ford was in no condition to undertake the lengthy fight scene that was written for him and the villain. Rather than losing a day of filming and a lot of money, Ford suggested that he just shoot the villain instead. There are literally hundreds of stories like this, where scenes were altered because of a happy accident or simple necessity.

Whatever the route taken, it is a very difficult trip that few screenplays are able to make, and of the small percentage of scripts that do become films, an even smaller number of those films are successful enough to reach a large audience. Writing a film is a difficult, often thankless and unglamorous undertaking. Think of all the films you have seen. How many writers can you name?

Review

- Most screenplays follow one of three structures: climactic, three-act, or circular.
- Screen writers must ask themselves the question: "What is different about today?" in order to clearly communicate the beginning of the story.

Key Terms

Narrative

Exposition

Rising Action

Climax

Falling Action

Stasis

Chapter 7

Trigger Event

Point of no return

Reversal

Adapted Screenplay

Original Screenplay

Genre

Conflict

All film genres go through a four-stage development process: primitive stage, classical stage, revisionist stage, parody stage.

NARRATIVE

CHAPTER 8

Film narrative is widely regarded as having two primary components: the actual story being told and the way that the story is being told (form). We discussed this briefly in Chapter 2 when we discussed realism, classicism, and formalism. These are the styles of film narrative. As previously discussed, the story may be one style while the form may be another.

The Film Spectrum

Realism	Classicism	Formalism
Documentaries "Day in the life"	Most fiction films Standard story and narratives	Experimental Avant-garde

© Kendall Hunt Publishing Company.

THOUGHTS AND IDEAS

One of the chief difficulties inherent in film is how to express thoughts and ideas through a form that is primarily visual. As in literature, there are a number of ways that film can present abstract ideas, but the primary ones are symbols, metaphors, motifs, allegories, and allusions.

SYMBOLS

In film, a **symbol** can be an actual symbol, but more often it is something in the scene that has implications beyond its simple existence. The same object can be a symbol for myriad ideas based on its context and use in a scene. We have discussed in previous chapters how colors can be symbols. Red can represent love and passion as well as anger and pain, depending on how it is used. The same is true for an object like fire; it can symbolize passion and romance or anger and destruction.

In *Run, Lola, Run* there is a recurring symbol of a circle. The film begins with a medium shot of a cuckoo clock. It is a circular clock, as all clocks in the film are. This echoes the circular structure of the film while emphasizing the importance of time always slipping away. The circular structure of the story and the time limit present in the film are reinforced. Early in the film we see a cartoon of a roulette dealer starting the ball in play, which also starts Lola spinning, trying to figure out whom she can turn to for the money. The roulette wheel echoes both the circular nature of the film and the underlying theme of the randomness of life events. The film explores how different our lives might be, based on changing just a few small events. This is equally true of roulette. Throughout the film, we see circles on top of circles next to circles, each one symbolizing something slightly different while reinforcing the overriding idea of chance.

METAPHOR

A **metaphor** is comparison that is not literally true. If people say they are "heart-broken," they do not mean that their heart has actually been broken and is no longer working. In film, metaphors can be through images that are not literally true but show us an image from which we can draw an idea. In the film *Trainspotting*, a character swims through his own filth and excrement to retrieve a suppository full of heroin. We are not meant to believe that the character actually swam in the disgusting mess. It is a metaphor showing how strong and desperate his addiction has become.

From Trainspotting, an unforgettable metaphor for addiction.

Motif

A **motif** is the most difficult technique to identify. It is so deeply ingrained into the film itself that it can be difficult to spot, even on multiple viewings. It is an object or image that is repeated throughout the film without drawing attention to it. For example, a film may have a recurring image of showing half a face, other half obscured in shadow or by an object. The motif is subtly illustrating the fact that we never truly show our full selves to others, only allowing them to see the part of ourselves that we want them to see.

Allegory

An allegory is an overt and somewhat simplistic technique in which a character or situation is connected to an idea. The most obvious example is when you have characters whose name tells us exactly what they are to represent. A large number of horror films have Death appear as an actual character. No subtlety here—the character clearly represents the idea.

Here Crusading knight Antonius Block literally plays chess with Death in Ingmar Bergman's The Seventh Seal. *This scene was given an homage in the teen comedy* Bill and Ted's Bogus Journey *when they play Death in a number of games including Twister.*

Allusion

The final technique is an allusion. This is when a film makes reference to a well-known event, film, or person. An allusion can be subtle and understated. The film *My Own Private Idaho* borrows heavily from Shakespeare's *Henry IV*, and many films have "Christ figures" or draw allusions to the Garden of Eden. While not overt, they do connect on some level with audiences that, by understanding the allusion, can draw conclusions not readily evident in the story itself.

A more obvious and overt allusion is called an **homage.** This is when the story directly references the event, person, or work. Most often it is referencing another film. This is usually done out of respect for the previous work, even if it is being spoofed. In the action film parody *Hot Shots! Part Deux*, the romantic leads re-enact the famous spaghetti scene from *The Lady and the Tramp*. The staircase scene in *The Untouchables* is an homage to the Odessa Steps scene from *The Battleship Potemkin*.

POINT OF VIEW

In literature as in film, there are four kinds of point of view: omniscient, first person, third person, objective. Point of view refers to from whom the story comes. Who is the narrator or, if there is no narrator, who is "telling" the story? The point of view gives us the person or persons through whose eyes we watch the events unfold.

Omniscient

The omniscient point of view is by far the most common view in all of film. We are watching the story through the eyes of someone who is not involved in the action but can see the action taking place in multiple locations and dealing with multiple characters. This view provides the audience members with all the information they need to understand the action of the film and can give insight into the minds of multiple characters.

The omniscient narrator is almost a necessity in film since every time the director changes the angle or distance of a shot it changes the audience's point of view. This is much harder to do in the other points of view.

First Person

First person narrators are directly involved in the action of the story. They may be objective observers who have enough distance from the situation to be trusted and believed, like the *Lord of the Rings*' benevolent elf-queen narrator Galadriel, who has been around for centuries and has seen all that has happened while maintaining an elf's detachment. Other times, the first persons become directly involved in the story and we may or may not be able to trust them, like *Sunset Boulevard*'s Joe Gillis, who gets pulled into Norma Desmond's world so completely that it kills him, or *Memento*'s Leonard, who has lost his short-term memory and can remember only snatches of moments or information that he has written down.

Third person

Third person narration is much trickier to pull off than omniscient or first person. In a third person point of view, we are allowed to see inside the mind of a single character but not in a way that suggests that this character is the one telling the story. This technique was used often in nineteenth-century novels and can be seen most clearly in the film adaptations of those films. In *Pride and Prejudice* we see the world through the eyes of Elizabeth Bennet as she falls in love with the wealthy Mr. Darcy. We never see into the lives of the other characters, but the film is clearly not told from Elizabeth's point of view; rather, it is told by someone else who appears to have received the version of the story from Elizabeth.

OBJECTIVE

The completely objective point of view is totally detached from the action, even more so than the omniscient point of view. The objective never shows us the inner thoughts of any character and chooses rather to present the information and allow the audience to interpret it as they will. Some of the earliest films fit this point of view. They actually set up a camera and let the action unfold: *Arrival of a Train* and *Workers Leaving the Lumiere Factory* are true documentaries that show us the action without comment.

Review

There are four primary points-of-view for a story's narrative:

1. Omniscient: sees all, knows all, tells all.
2. First person: the point of view of a character involved in the story.
3. Third person: allows insight into one specific character (the protagonist) without that character being the story teller.
4. Objective: presents the information as a disinterested observer, allows no insight into any character; common in early documentary films.

Key Terms

Symbol

Metaphor

Motif

Allegory

Allusion

Homage

ACTING

CHAPTER 9

The most easily identifiable aspect of film is acting. Acting deals with creating believable characters who participate in the action of the film. Actors are the most visible technicians working on a movie and, as a result, receive the greatest amount of fame, recognition, and criticism.

LEVELS OF ACTING

There are four types of actors or levels of acting in film: extras, non-professional actors, professional actors, and stars. Each level has its own specific purpose and specific challenges. The first two levels are actors whom we rarely notice, and the last two can often make or break a movie.

EXTRAS

The people moving around in the background of crowd scenes who have no lines or defined characters are extras. Extras are glorified scenery. Their sole purpose is to fill out the scenes so the audience gets the sense of scale for the events taking place. Extras require no training or resume'. They are most often people off the street who are brought in and told to stand here or walk there, as the case may be. They are usually hired for one day of shooting at a time, with their call being a 12-hour period in which they will be filmed in a scene. Extras often bring their own clothing for the shoot (if the scene is "modern day"). They are paid a small stipend and provided meals for the time they are on set. They receive minimal attention from the director and other actors and are regarded almost as live furniture.

People walking in and out of the bank prior to the robbery in *Dog Day's Afternoon* would be considered extras and be paid accordingly. If the crowd scene is large enough and already part of some other event, the extras may not be paid. In the movie *Rudy*, the final game footage was filmed during halftime of a Notre Dame football game. Those who were in attendance for the game were used as the crowd for the footage but were not paid for their time.

Non-professional Actors

In some cases, extras are called on to take small speaking roles. These are usually parts with only one or two lines that are necessary for the film but not large enough or challenging enough for the casting director to seek out a professional for the role. Non-professional actors are those with speaking lines in a film who do not make their living as actors. Often they are the same people who are asked to be extras. If actors have any spoken lines in the film, they must join the actor's union, Actor's Equity. This changes what they are paid, the amount of time they can be required to be on set, as well as other union contract issues.

Members of Actor's Equity will receive two to three times the amount of money that extras will make, and will receive it for any time they work on the film, even if they have lines in only one scene. A membership fee is required to join the union, and members must pay a percentage of their income from the film to the union. It usually works out that as long as these actors work more than one day in the year, they will come out ahead by joining the union. In the film *Naked Gun: From the files of Police Squad!* someone in the crowd at a baseball game shouts, "It's Enrico Palazzo!" This is a non-professional actor.

Professional Actors

Professional actors are those who have received training to be an actor and who make their living as an actor. These can be character actors whom you see in many films but can't remember their name, or actors who play more supporting roles and don't have the power and prestige of a star. Most identifiable actors in a film are professional actors. Technically, stars are professional actors as well, but they are on an entirely different level than your standard professional actor.

Stars

There are two kinds of stars: actor stars and personality stars. What separates a star from a professional actor is the ability to get a film made and to carry a movie. A star is someone the audience goes to see regardless of the film. If a person is going to a movie and says, "I'm going to see the new Brad Pitt movie," that establishes Brad Pitt as a star.

Actor star Actor stars are those who are viewed as stars because of their abilities as actors. These are stars who tend to do films that receive critical acclaim and are nominated for Academy Awards.

Personality star Personality stars are actors whom audiences go to see because of their personality or looks rather than their acting ability. Action stars tend to fall into this category.

In the 1980s, 1990s, and early 2000s, the star system was going strong. Most films were star-driven and actors were able to draw salaries of $10 million to $20 million. Actor stars like Jack Nicholson, Meryl Streep, Robert DeNiro, Nicole Kidman, Tom Hanks, and others were routinely recognized with Academy Awards, while personality stars like Julia Roberts, Bruce Willis, Sylvester Stallone, and others raked in huge paydays, scoring with tremendously successful movies. In the last several years, though, the industry has shifted from star-driven vehicles to event movies. While Robert Downey Jr. could be argued to be a star, his films are successful more because they are the "new *Iron Man* movie" and the "new *Sherlock Holmes* film" than because they are the "new Robert Downey Jr. movie."

Acting Levels

Extras	Non-professional
Off the street Living scenery	Extras w/speaking part Must join actors' union
Professional	**Star**
Makes a living acting Appears in movies mostly in supporting roles	Must be able to open a movie, carry a movie and get a movie made

Image courtesy of Jason Gonzalez

STAR SYSTEM

What does it take to be a star? There are essentially three things that make an actor a star: the ability to open a movie, the ability to carry a movie, and the ability to get a movie made.

OPENING A MOVIE

Most films make the largest part of their income from the first two or three weeks the movie is in theaters. This is where most movies break even. If an actor is a big enough star to get audiences to come those first few weekends, the studio is much more likely to be able to turn a profit on the film. A film that opens strong can be financially successful even if it is not good. Audiences spend their money before they realize the film is bad, and the studio makes a profit. An actor who can bring out an audience regardless of the film's content or quality becomes very valuable and can then ask for more money.

CARRYING A MOVIE

The ability to carry a movie has two parts: financial (personality star) and artistic (actor star). A star who can carry a movie will appear in most of the scenes in the movie and will be called on to provide the key speeches and memorable moments of the film.

Actors who carry a movie will consistently bring the movie significant financial return compared to the cost of their salaries. In the 90s, Julia Roberts and Mel Gibson were huge stars and carried many movies, but due to their inflated salaries, they didn't provide a huge return on their investment. In today's Hollywood, most of the top returners are actors who find themselves in big-event movies. Shia LeBeouf and Daniel Radcliffe would not be considered stars, yet they each return more than $100 of box office for every dollar of salary they receive.

If a movie doesn't open strong, it must have **legs**—it must continue making money for an extended period of time. The best example of a film with legs is *Titanic*. While this was not a star-driven movie, it became the highest grossing film ever at the time of its release despite making only $28 million on its opening weekend. More than 200 films have had better openings than Titanic, but none have had its legs.

GETTING MOVIES MADE

In Chapter 7, on screenplay, we discussed how a script gets turned into a movie. One of the chief deciding factors for studios is, of course: What is the chance we can make money from it? A true star is an actor who can get a script into production merely by being contracted to appear in a film. If the studio executives view an actor as a "can't miss money maker," they will be much more likely to green-light a film if that actor is attached to the film. An actor like George Clooney, who enjoys making smaller movies that are focused more on story than special effects, can get that small movie made because of the financial and critical successes of his larger films, such as *Ocean's 11* and *The Perfect Storm*.

THE ACTOR'S CRAFT

Acting is a combination of ability and technique. While many non-actors believe that memorizing lines is the actor's most difficult task, what separates the great actors is the ability to create believable and relatable characters. Audiences may not always be able to tell why they think an actor is doing a poor job, but they "know it when they see it." Think of the actors who receive the most critical acclaim, the ones you most enjoy watching perform. What is it that they have in common? They are natural and they seem to be very comfortable in the character they have created. Audiences will forget that they are watching a particular actor and get drawn into the character being portrayed.

There are many acting styles and methods used to portray a character. Much in the same way that the narrative can run from realistic to formalistic, acting styles can run from realistic to expressionistic. A large majority of acting styles, however, stay down near the realistic end of the spectrum. Actors most often try to create characters who seem realistic so audiences can relate to them and the situations they face during the action of the film.

Spencer Tracy, who was the first actor to win back-to-back Academy Awards for Best Actor, said that his method of acting was to "remember my lines and try not to bump into the furniture." He didn't do a lot of background work and study of a character. Instead, he found the "person" in the character and went from there. Funny lines aside, Tracy probably spent time thinking about what his character was feeling and why he was doing what he was doing.

STANISLAVSKI'S METHOD

Human beings only ever do or say anything because they want something in return. Whether they want to make someone like them, love them, leave them alone or pass them the salt, there is always a reason that they do and say what they do and say. In the late nineteenth and early twentieth centuries, an actor at the Moscow Art Theater named Konstantin Stanislavki found that he didn't like the way that actors were performing. He felt they weren't genuine. Acting at the time was what you would find in early silent films. Actors would make specific gestures to signify anger or sadness or fear. Stanislavski felt, quite correctly, that real people didn't behave that way. He developed a new acting style that completely altered the way actors performed. His method is complex enough to take up three books, but the major elements of his method called for actors to put themselves inside the minds of the characters they were portraying and try to truly understand their thoughts and feelings in a way that no one had ever done before.

One of the tools that he developed for accomplishing this was what he called the "magic if." The basic premise is that the actor asks, "IF this were happening to me, how would I feel and what would I do?" If what the actor would do and what the character did were different, it was then up to the actor to explore why the character made a different choice.

Stanislavski's method has become so pervasive that few actors in the world today do not use some portion of his teachings in their craft.

STRASBURG AND THE ACTOR'S STUDIO

It took a while for Stanislavski's teachings to make it from the stage of the Moscow Art Theater to Hollywood. In 1947, The Actor's Studio was opened in New York as a place for actors to come and learn their craft from experts in the field. Many famous actors, from Marlon Brando to Dustin Hoffman to Robert DeNiro to Marilyn Monroe, came through The Actor's Studio. Lee Strasburg was one of the chief teachers at the studio, and he taught Stanislavski's method to his students—sort of. Strasburg focused on having the actors immerse themselves in the lives of their characters, but rather than having them ask the "magic if," he taught them to experience first-hand what their characters were feeling. This led to some tremendous performances and some unusual on-set experiences.

Dustin Hoffman was in the film *Marathon Man*, and in one particular scene, his character is supposed to be exhausted from running a marathon and then being sleep-deprived for several days. Hoffman reportedly went without sleep for 3 days prior to shooting the scene and went for a 10-mile run on the morning of the filming in order to fully experience what his character was feeling. His co-star in the scene, Laurence Olivier, was asked later what he thought of Hoffman's choice and said, "Terribly noble of the lad, but hasn't he heard of acting?"

ACTING IN FILM

While a large number of actors will shift between television, live theater, and film, each medium requires a very different way of creating a character. The first major difference comes in the subtlety that an actor can use in film that does not work on stage, for example. When acting on stage, actors have to make big movements and broad gestures so they can be seen sometimes as much as a hundred or more feet away. In film, an actor can use smaller gestures and movements because the camera can bring the audience to within a few inches of the actor in some cases. Sir Laurence Olivier, widely regarded as one of the greatest actors of his generation, struggled when he first started acting in films because he was so accustomed to projecting his characters in a larger-than-life way for the stage. It took him a few films to get used to acting for the camera.

A second difference comes from the way each performance is rehearsed and presented. On stage, actors rehearse six to eight weeks, going over all the scenes dozens of times, while in film there may be very little or no rehearsal ahead of time. Actors in a live play learn their parts in order and must remember everything for the entire time they are working on a show. Actors in a movie film scenes out of sequence and in short bursts. They can afford to "learn it and flush it." They learn the lines and the scene for the day or days that they will be shooting it, and then can let it go and move on to a new scene.

One of the reasons that rehearsal is more important to live theater than to film is due to the live nature of the performance. A scene is rehearsed over and over to make sure that the actors know it by heart, because there is no room for even a small mistake when performing live. On a film set, it is expected that every scene will be filmed multiple times whether there is a mistake or a director gives an acting note or the scene is shot from a different angle. Multiple takes are a given, so there is less necessity to have the scene perfectly ready to be performed as soon as the cameras start rolling.

Acting in film is a very different experience, too, because of the way a movie is shot. Because of the nature of a shot, an actor may be talking to a camera or to a person just off camera who is not the actor who appears in the scene. A quiet romantic scene may be difficult to focus on because there is a large camera a foot or two away, a boom mic, lighting instruments, a director, a cinematographer, and a crew of 10 to 15 technicians all crowding around staring at the actors performing the scene. It can be unnerving and can take some getting used to.

As special effects have improved, acting opposite large green screens or technicians holding broom handles has increased. Actors in science fiction films will often not see the monstrous aliens that they are battling throughout the film until they see the final cut of the movie. Instead, they will be acting in a studio in front of a large green screen with someone holding something to indicate where the head of the alien is in the shot. It can be difficult to get worked up with anger or fear while looking at a stick.

While the technical aspects of filming a movie can be a challenge to actors, they can allow filmmakers to do things with actors that they would never be able to do otherwise. If an actor is going to be a hero and win the maiden, one thing he needs to be is tall and handsome. In film, all he really needs to be is handsome. Directors can make an actor seem to be much taller than he actually is by the way they set up the shots or what they do out of view of the camera.

Chuck Norris, Tom Cruise, and Sylvester Stallone, just to name a few, are not tall men. Cruise and Norris are actually below-average height, but by always filming them from a low angle, the audience believes them to be taller. In *Rocky IV*, Stallone stands face-to-face with actor Dolph Lundgren, who is some 8 or so inches taller than him. They wanted Lundgren's character Ivan Drago to seem intimidating, but having him that much taller than Rocky would have made it difficult to keep him in the shot.

CASTING

The first and most difficult task for any actor is to get the role. When actors are first starting out, they may audition hundreds of times before they land a role. It is a brutal, heart-breaking, and thankless business for most actors. According to some statistics, 90% of all actors are not employed as actors at any given moment. Getting that first break can be difficult, and getting a second one depends entirely on what is done with the first.

Every actor, because of the body, face, or style, is a certain type. Types developed over 2,000 years of theater include: the hero and ingénue (young girl or love interest), conniving servant, greedy old man, braggart soldier, and many more. Some actors are physically attractive and are immediately typed as romantic leads. Others are not and become comic side-kicks or villains.

Type casting is when actors become so associated with a specific type that they are continually cast in that role. Adam Sandler has played the same man-child in *Happy Gilmore*, *Mr. Deeds*, *Big Daddy*, *The Waterboy*, and *Billy Madison*. Action stars like Sylvester Stallone and Arnold Schwarzeneggar have made entire careers out of playing essentially the same character over and over again. This is not to say that if someone becomes type cast, they are not good actors. Harrison Ford has played a similar role in 20+ films, as has Sean Connery. Once an actor has been type cast, though, it can be difficult to break out of that mold.

Casting against type is when actors have developed a "type" and then try a film that goes against that type. When they do, it is often unsuccessful because audiences have grown so accustomed to seeing these actors in a certain light that they don't want to see these actors change. Adam Sandler tries to do serious films periodically, like *Punch Drunk Love*, which was a critical and box-office failure. Schwarzeneggar and long-time serious actor Robert DeNiro were cast in comedies with different levels of success. Arnold's *Twins* was a mild success, but his turn as a pregnant man in *Junior* was a total dud. DeNiro's comic turns in the *Meet the Parents* and *Analyze This* series actually succeeded. Denzel Washington won an Academy Award when he was cast against type by playing a villain in *Training Day*.

Comedian Robin Williams was cast against type as a sad, serious, psychologist Sean Maguire. The result was an Academy Award for Best Actor in a Supporting Role.

Some actors work very hard not to be type cast to begin with. Both Johnny Depp and Brad Pitt were well on their way to a career as pretty-boy romantic leads. Depp began seeking out quirky, unusual roles where his good looks were hidden behind strange make-up and costumes from *Edward Scissorhands* to *Pirates of the Caribbean*. Depp fought hard not to become just another pretty face. Ironically, he has now become type cast as the quirky, unusual guy in strange make-up and weird costumes.

Pitt did several roles in a row where he played dark characters who were not attractive either physically or emotionally. His turns in *Kalifornia*, *12 Monkeys*, and *Seven* allowed him the opportunity to slide back and forth between mainstream romantic leads and dark, conflicted men.

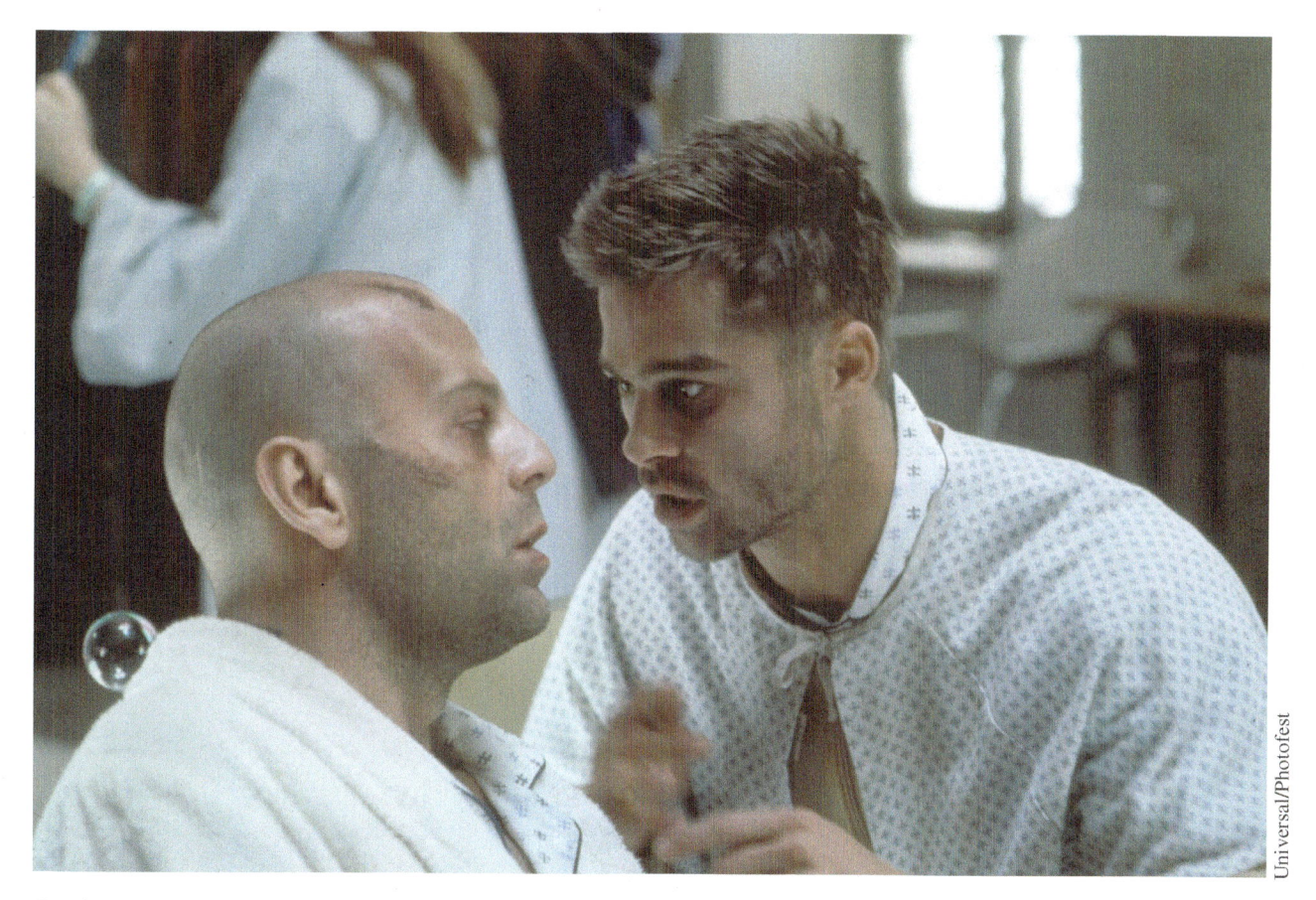

Brad Pitt's tour-de-force performance as an insane trust fund kid in 12 Monkeys allowed him to break out of any "type" he might have been developing into.

It is not only men who fight against becoming type cast. Charlize Theron began her career as a sex symbol in films such as *2 Days in the Valley*, *The Devil's Advocate*, and *Reindeer Games*. She was not being taken seriously as an actor because of her appearance, so in 2003 she took the role of female serial killer Aileen Wuornos in *Monster*. Like Pitt and Depp before her, she played a character who was physically and emotionally frightening. The result was the first of several Academy Award nominations and a win for Best Actress.

Ultimately, whatever the actor's method, whatever the actor's type, it comes down to creating a character that audiences can believe in and connect with—a real person. Whatever you may think of Stallone's later work, his performance in the original *Rocky* is a moving portrayal of an entirely relatable and believable character, and that is the goal that every actor hopes to achieve.

Charlize Theron was able to lose herself in the role of serial killer Aileen Wuornos.

Review

There are four levels of actors:

1. Extras
2. Non-Professional Actors
3. Professional Actors
4. Stars

A star can be either a personality star or an actor star but must have the ability to open a movie, carry a movie, and get a movie made in order to be considered a star.

Acting in film can be a very difficult and technical task with all the inherent obstacles of limited rehearsal—, filming out of order, location, scheduling, and large crews.

While there are many acting styles, most involve elements from the method created by Russian actor Konstantin Stanislavski.

Directors will often use actors who are famous for playing a specific kind of role. This is called type casting. If actors instead play a role that is opposite of what they usually play (a hero playing a villain, a comedian playing a serious role), it is called casting against type.

LIGHTING & SOUND

CHAPTER 10

In 1927 *The Jazz Singer* ushered in the new era of "talkies." It was the first film to include a soundtrack that provided simultaneous (synchronous) sound. Prior to the advent of synchronous sound all films had musical accompaniment in the theaters in which they were shown. In large cities they might have a full orchestra playing, while in small towns a single piano would play during the film.

ONE GIANT STEP BACK

Today sound is such an integral part of film that audiences can't even imagine films without it. However, when sound first came on the scene it caused more problems than it solved.

Money

Prior to "talkies," films were not big money-making ventures. This allowed them to be artistic and experimental, when filmmakers didn't have to worry about turning a profit they could do more or less what they wanted with their films; sound changed that. Suddenly investors in New York saw Hollywood as a new place to make money and they began spending wildly in an effort to get in on the ground floor and turn the biggest profit possible. This new profit motive for making films greatly reduced experimentation and exploration; it put people who knew little or nothing about film into decision-making positions. The result was that creativity was stifled in favor of making movies that "sell."

Sound

The process of recording sound onto film was also a major drawback early on. The camera made a significant amount of noise which microphones could pick up, so the camera and microphones had to be kept a distance apart, but not too far. This also meant that the actors weren't as free to move around as they used to be. They had to stay near to where the microphones were set, often inside a plant or a lamp or other easily disguised props. It reduced the amount of action in a film because chase scenes were difficult to record sound for; the end result was dialogue heavy movies with little action. Over time advances in sound helped to overcome many of these issues; a boom mic was developed so that actors could be recorded as they moved around the set.

Editing

Putting two strips of film together in order to edit a scene is a relatively easy process when there is no soundtrack. Once sound is added, however, it becomes much more difficult and time consuming. Since all sound was recorded synchronously at the time it meant that almost all editing was done at scene changes. It was as if film had moved back to the style of performing usually associated with a live stage show.

Nonsynchronous Sound

Most formalist directors preferred to use sound sparingly to allow them more creativity and flexibility. They also began using nonsynchronous sound, that is, sound that is recorded at a different time and place and added in at a later time. This process, called **dubbing**, quickly became a standard way of using sound in film.

Dubbing

Dubbing solved many of the problems inherent in synchronous sound recording. It allowed scenes to be shot at a distance and then sound added in later. It meant that chase scenes were once again possible making "talkies" less dialogue heavy.

Dubbing allows actors to come back into the studio after a scene has been shot and edited and add in their dialogue without having to worry about outside noise that the microphones may have picked up in the original filming. It meant that many mistakes or problems could be fixed in postproduction.

Foley

Actors recording their dialogue after the fact is dubbing; a foley artist adds in other atmospheric sounds that might have been lost, covered, or not available when the scene was originally filmed. If, for example, the scene involved a long shot of a young couple walking along a gravel road talking together and flirting lightly, the distance of the shot would mean that the dialog would have to be dubbed in later. It would also mean that other sounds would be recorded in the studio. Along with the sound of the couple walking on the gravel road, they might want the sound of birds singing in the trees perhaps they want to hear the breeze blowing. All of these would be added in by the foley artist.

Sound Effects

In today's films most sound effects are mixed in after the fact. Although the sound may have a source in the scene itself, they are added later because it is easier to get the exact sound that the director wants.

For example, in the television show *The X-Files* there was a character who has a weapon that looks like a space-age ice pick. When the character activates the weapon it extends into position. The director wanted a specific sound to accompany the weapon sliding out. The sound editors tried a number of sounds but ultimately the director made the sound he wanted by clicking a pen.

Action and science fiction films especially use a massive amount of sound effects. Many of the technologies in these films don't exist in the real world, so the sound associated with them must be developed by the sound mixer. Not only is the sound developed but also the relative volume of the sound, the length of the sound, and more all have to be decided on. The louder a sound the more forceful it feels to the audience; the softer the more delicate it feels. A higher-pitched sound effect has more suspense and generates more fear, whereas a lower pitch seems more solemn. A fast tempo has the same effect as a loud and higher-pitched effect, while a slower tempo fits more naturally with softer, lower-pitched effects.

If we take the sound effect from the famous shower scene in *Psycho*, we find that it is loud, high-pitched, and fast tempo. This provokes in the audience a feeling of suspense and fear which works perfectly with the scene.

Much in the same way that the director works with scenic and costume designers they work with sound mixers. They will give the mixer an idea of what they want the sound to be, the mixer will create it, and the director will provide feedback until they have achieved the exact sound desired.

POINT OF VIEW

Nonsynchronous sound can be presented to represent synchronous sound. This is called point of view. In filming, a point-of-view shot is one in which the audience is shown what the character is looking at. In sound, point of view allows the audience to hear what the character is hearing. The primary reason this is used is to illustrate that the character is hearing a distorted version of the real sound. In *Rocky*, during the boxing scenes we shift back and forth from Rocky's point of view to "real" sound. When we are hearing what Rocky is hearing the sound is far away and distorted because he has been hit repeatedly in the head and ears. In *Saving Private Ryan* after a loud explosion next to a soldier damages his hearing, we are given his audio point of view. This immerses us further into the roiling chaos of the Normandy invasion.

MUSIC

Music in film can be sound that is heard by the characters or it can be the background soundtrack of a scene. Music that is heard by the characters can be from the radio, concerts, or the like. They add to the atmosphere of the scene and can be used to comment on the scene. In *Apocalypse Now*, Lt. Colonel Kilgore leads a helicopter attack on a village in Vietnam. He has Flight of the Valkyries played at full volume during the attack to inspire his men and to frighten the villagers.

Background or **incidental** music can't be heard by the characters in the scene and is used to create mood or atmosphere. This is the most common type of music used in film. There are literally thousands of examples where music is used to enhance the mood or tone of a scene. From romantic music when two people are falling in love to inspirational themes as the heroes ready themselves for the big battle, modern film is filled with incidental music that does not simply add to the film experience but increases it exponentially.

If the music is used repeatedly it can become thematic. In *Raiders of the Lost Ark*, there is a very specific piece of music that plays whenever Indiana Jones sets out to right a wrong. In *Jaws*, the menacing theme music is used to build suspense and let us know that somewhere a giant great white shark is lurking.

MUSICALS

One of the longest lasting genres in film is the movie musical. The basic premise of musicals is that the characters are experiencing feelings that are so strong that they can only be expressed by breaking into song and choreographed dance routines. Like other genres musicals can fall at virtually any place along the spectrum from realism to formalism. Realistic musicals try to work the song and dance routines into the plot as though it was part of their daily life. Many of these musicals are backstage stories that take place in theaters. Kiss Me Kate, the musical version of Shakespeare's Taming of the Shrew is an example of a realistic musical.

Try watching Rocky's inspiring training montage without the accompanying music, it falls completely flat.

A formalistic musical, which is what most musicals are, do not try to justify the song and dance. They embrace the presentational style of musicals and unapologetically jump into the songs and dance numbers. The recent movie musical *Les Miserables* does not try to explain why young revolutionaries would sing while they are trying to beat back government soldiers.

THE ACTOR'S VOICE

The actor's voice is a key element to the sound of a film. The *Star Wars* series of films has a litany of characters who are enhanced by the way their voices are used. Darth Vader's deep resonant voice is so important to his character that James Earl Jones was hired to play the voice while another actor played the physical incarnation of the character. If Vader's voice was high and raspy it would not work nearly as well.

In addition to the quality of the actor's voice the way in which they say their lines can greatly affect the way the scenes are interpreted. An actor can put emphasis on different words changing the meaning of what they said: **I** will call you or I **will** call you or I will **call** you or I will call **you**. The way a line is spoken can also be altered by the tone or volume used. When Luke Skywalker is told he must work on the farm, he whines, "but I wanted to go to Tashi station to get some power converters." His whining establishes him as immature and unprepared for what the galaxy has in store for him.

Tempo is the speed and rate at which the actor speaks. This can include pausing for effect or speaking more rapidly. In the early days of sound, some directors tried to offset the large amount of dialogue by having actors speak more rapidly. This worked well for gangster films in particularly as the action seems to moving more quickly due to the rapid style of dialogue.

Characters can come from any of number of locations and the way that those characters speak can be affected by where they are from. **Dialect** is another word for the accent with which a person speaks, whether the accent is from a specific region or country. Different dialects have different connotations for audiences. For whatever reason, Hollywood has decided that the proper British dialect is perfect for cold, calculating villains. The southern dialect is poetic and works well for sultry women and proper men. The danger arises when dialects are used improperly or unnecessarily. George Lucas got in trouble for *Star Wars Episode 1* for making Jar Jar Binks speak in a cross between Pidgin and Jamaican dialects, having the Trade Federation members speak with heavy Japanese accents, and making slave trader Watto sound Jewish.

The text of a film, as we have discussed, is found in the script; it is what the characters say. **Subtext** is what the characters mean when they say what they say. For example, a couple may be having an argument when one of them shouts, "I am leaving," but they don't leave. They didn't mean that they were leaving, what they actually meant is the subtext. The opening scene of Quentin Tarantino's *Inglorious Basterds* is nearly 20 minutes of subtext. The Nazi officer appears to be talking about daily events, but there is clearly much more to what he is saying.

Star Wars *introduced the lovable robot R2–D2, who speaks only in beeps and whistles, yet the audience knows exactly what he is thinking at all times.*

A director or screen writer may choose to have information delivered to the audience by using a **voice-over**. A voice-over occurs when a character, sometimes a narrator, is speaking without being seen. They are often providing expositional information or insight into a character's thoughts. The original version of *Blade Runner* had a number of voice-overs throughout the film. These not only gave the audience Decker's thoughts and feelings but it also added to the Film Noir tone of the film as a whole.

Although sound originally seemed to be both a blessing and a curse, the advances of technology over the last 80+ years have allowed it to become an integral part of the film experience. All a viewer has to do to fully grasp the importance of sound is to turn the volume off and turn on the closed captioning while watching a film. The experience will be vastly different and likely not nearly as enjoyable.

LIGHTING

Lighting is an essential element used to enhance the mise-en-scéne of every moment of a film. Lighting can be used to establish the mood and atmosphere of a scene or film. It provides texture and dimension, and can hide or reveal key areas inside a shot. It can move the plot along, build suspense, and evoke strong emotions. Lighting can direct the audience's attention as much as editing or camera movement.

In film, lighting is either ambient or incidental. **Ambient light** is any light that is already present in the space. This can be practical lights like candles or lamps and natural light like the sun or moon. **Incidental light** is anything added to the scene by the film maker.

Goals

Lighting has essentially four goals: 1) establish mood or feeling; 2) create an image with aesthetic beauty; 3) provide depth and perspective; and most obviously, 4) allow the location and action of the scene to be visible to the audience.

Styles

Throughout the history of film there have been many kinds of lighting techniques used. Some of the earliest styles were born out of necessity due to the limitations of the technology of the time.

High-key lighting is a style of lighting with very low lighting ratio. That is, there is very little difference in the amount of light throughout the shot. High-key lighting provides an evenly lit scene with very few shadows. This was used often in the early days because film did not handle high-ratio lighting very well. Today, this style is used to create an upbeat or comic atmosphere where things are sunny, bright, and safe.

Low-key lighting is, as it sounds, the opposite of high-key lighting. The lighting ratio is much higher with bright areas contrasted with darker ones. In this style, there is usually only one light source and it is used to accentuate the contours of objects and create significant shadows. Low-key lighting was made popular by Film Noir and is used in many suspense and horror films today.

Three-point lighting is by far the most commonly used lighting style in film. The first "point" is the **key light**. This is a bright light that is shone on the primary or key element of the scene; what we would call the dominant in mise-en-scéne. It is set up at a 45-degree angle from the dominant and provides bright light, dark shadow, and a sense of depth to the shot.

The second point is the **fill light**. This is a softer light that is usually about half the strength of the key light. This intensity can be adjusted through the use of a smaller bulb or by using a filter or scrim (sheer fabric) in front of the light. It is placed on the opposite side of the dominant from the key light at about a 30-degree angle. The fill light "fills" in the space and diminishes the harsh shadows created by the key light.

The third and final point is the **back light**. This light is positioned behind the dominant to highlight it while also providing a sense of depth and dimension to the scene. It is most often placed directly opposite the key light for greatest effectiveness.

Standard Three-Point Lighting

#3 Back Light

Object

#1 Key Light

#2 Fill Light

KEY TERMS

Synchronous sound

Nonsynchronous sound

Dubbing

Foley

Sound effects

Point-of-view sound

Incidental music

Subtext

Ambient light

Incidental light

High-key lighting

Low-key lighting

Chapter 10

Three-Point lighting

Key light

Fill light

Back light

THE DIGITAL AGE

CHAPTER 11

As we have moved further and further into the 21st century the name "film" has become a less and less accurate description of what we see on the screens at the Cineplex or televisions or smart phones. For the first hundred or so years of the medium all movies were made on photo chemical film; now an increasing number of movies are being recorded digitally. The digital technology has improved to the point where deciding which format to record on is a legitimate debate. So let us look at both the history of digital recording as well as how it compares to photo chemical film.

DIGITAL DEVELOPMENT

In the late 1960s Bell Labs developed the first CCD chip. CCD (charge-coupled device) chips allowed for the transfer of an electronic charge from one storage capacitor to the next. The charge was represented by the movement of certain elements on the capacitor called pixels.

In the 1970s Sony realized that the CCD chips could be used to transfer images and began using them in electronic cameras. As the decade progressed the technology improved, though the only ones using the camera were professional photographers.

As we discussed back in **Chapter 1**, by the 1980s digital cameras had become consumer-friendly. They were small enough and inexpensive enough for just about anyone to use them. Also in that decade the first digital editing equipment was developed. This meant that something could be filmed and edited in a far shorter time.

In 1995 a group of Danish filmmakers came together to develop the **Dogme 95** manifesto. This was a way of making films focused on the traditional values of story, acting, and theme while excluding the increased importance given to elaborate special effects. As part of their manifesto the group would produce their films by using only hand-held video cameras and digital editing equipment. The 1998 film *Celebration* was the first Dogme 95 film and it would go on to win the Jury Prize at the Cannes Film Festival.

In 2002, the first major studio film to be shot entirely with a digital camera, *Star Wars Episode II: Attack of the Clones*, may have signaled the beginning of the end for photo chemical film stock as the primary format for motion pictures. The number of films shot partially and completely on digital video has increased exponentially over the last decade. In the next section, we will look at some of the reasons why digital video is growing so quickly.

FILM VS DIGITAL

To begin with let's look at the way in which each format records images. In a film camera, light enters through the lens and hits a frame of film in an emulsion of silver halide crystals. The crystals change when the light hits them and they are turned into silver upon development (which is probably where the name "silver screen" comes from).

As we discussed earlier in the chapter, a digital camera has a chip with a sensor full of millions of pixels. Light hits the sensor and creates individual electronic charges; this is the digital data, the image that we see on the screen.

Image Quality

The quality of film images has changed little over the last 120 years. The change from black and white to color was the primary way in which the film quality was improved but most other improvements to the image were a result of advances in lighting, editing, and special effects. What an image shot on film provides that digital does not are texture, grain, and a certain amount of grit. This becomes a part of the mise-en-scéne in a subtle way. It is another element of the movie.

Conversely, digital images have no grit or texture; you are not even aware that it is there. Today, with the advances in technology the digital image is clear, almost pristine. The major drawback of shooting on video in the 1990s was that the shots looked "amateurish" like they were home videos. They lacked a depth of field that you would get from a film camera. This aesthetic worked well for the Dogme 95 group who wanted a more intimate almost documentary look to their films. The idea that their films were practically home movies was appealing to them. However, for mainstream motion pictures and the industry as a whole this was not something they wanted to replicate in their commercial films.

As the technology improved both in filming and in editing the image became more professional, and although it does not offer the same visual depth of field as film, it is close enough that the other advantages that it offers make it a viable alternative to film.

Cost

If video looked cheap and amateurish, why did anyone want to use it? First, digital video does allow the filmmaker to generate a much larger amount of footage since it is so much cheaper than film stock. Even today, the comparable amount of film stock is approximately 300 times the cost of a memory card for digital video camera. What this translates to is the ability to experiment more during the filming process. It means that the director can film anything that they can think of and then decide what works and what doesn't in the editing room. It allows for much greater creativity because they can have so much more footage to choose from.

Shooting Schedule

One of the parts of the filming process that takes the most time, and therefore more money, is setting up each individual shot. Film stock, as we discussed back in **Chapter 2**, requires additional lighting, particularly when using slow stock film as most major motion pictures do. The time, effort, and personnel required to set up a single shot, even indoors, can be massive. It is not unusual for a single scene to require 12 hours to shoot. A digital video camera doesn't need the extra lighting, personnel, and setup. A director can get a group of actors to the location of the shot and within a few minutes begin filming. This means that less time is spent on preparation for the scenes and more time can be spent on the actual scenes themselves.

The size and flexibility of the digital camera allows for more intimate camera work as you can get much closer and need far less light than film stock. It means that you cannot only get shots that might be much harder to set up in the past but that you could even shoot with multiple cameras at the same time, as they do in television, saving time and money.

Another major difference from shooting with a film camera was the length of time that you could film without stopping. A film camera runs on a magazine of film that can record for about 10 minutes. After that time, shooting has to stop while the camera is reloaded with a new magazine, everything is reset and filming can begin again. A video camera can shoot from 40 minutes to two hours without needing to be reloaded. As a result, even more time can be saved and more work can be done every single day of shooting. This greatly altered the way filming took place. Before, actors could take a break, go back to their trailers and relax or regroup. Now, they have to keep going for a much longer time. Actor Robert Downey Jr. was so thrown the first time that he worked on a movie shot on a video camera that he started leaving mason jars full of urine around the set to emphasize the need for periodic breaks.

During the first 80 years of film one inherent problem during the filming process was that when a shot was filmed only the camera operator and the director of photography knew exactly what it looked like. The director and everyone else had to wait for the "rushes" or the developed footage from the day of shooting. If the director didn't like the way the shot turned out the choice was to reshoot the scene the following day or accept it and hope that you could make it better in the editing. Today, the results from a digital camera can be viewed in real time on a large-screen TV or, at the very least, immediately after the scene has been shot. This can be both a blessing and a curse. Everyone can have a very clear idea of what the scene looks like but it also allows for everyone to offer their opinion and "overthink" or "overshoot" a scene in an attempt to be absolutely perfect.

So, if digital cameras can offer all of these benefits, why would anyone still shoot with film? Nostalgia? Maybe some people choose to photo chemical film for that reason; because it is the way that Hitchcock or John Ford or Kurosawa made movies. For most who still choose to shoot on film it is because of the way it looks and the artistry that can be created through an adept manipulation of the film stock. There is still something solid and tactile and serious about making a movie with a film camera. It feels professional like the filmmaker is more of an artist. As much as the resolution with digital cameras have improved they are still not as effective as film at capturing the whole breadth and depth and texture of a scene. Digital cameras still present a more sterile, flat world than a film camera.

Editing

The first real digital editing machine was developed in 1980 and it completely altered how films were edited. The old way of joining two pieces of film together was incredibly time consuming. As we mentioned in the chapter on editing, films prior to the 1980s had fewer cuts than the films that came later. One of the reasons for that was the difficulty and time-consuming nature of the process.

Digital editing is not only much faster than the old film editing process, but it also allows for much quicker and easier manipulation of the image for special effects. There is a famous picture of George Lucas surrounded by all of the models of starships, planets, the Death Star, and such from the original Star Wars film. Lucas appears to be adrift in a sea of clay and plastic models. A similar picture was taken more than 30 years later with Lucas and all of the models used for Star Wars Episode 2; it is just George Lucas standing alone in front of a green screen. This is the difference between film and digital special effects.

On film, you need to actually record small-scale models doing whatever it is supposed to be doing. Often layers of film have to be combined by overlaying the original scene with one level of special effects and then another and then another. This can lead to small continuity mistakes and image degradation. Today, in an effort to overcome some of the limitations of photo chemical film editing a movie will be converted to a digital format in order to add special effects and then converted back to film. This can be very expensive so it is generally used only in movies with an extreme number of special effects where the time and effort saved outweighs the cost of multiple conversions.

Digital editing allows all of the special effects to be added later by computer. This allows a level of precision and ease that film editing does not. For example, the color balance of photo chemical film is created by a colorist who, in conjunction with the director, decides how the scene should look and then has to immerse the film for a different amount of time to get each of the different kinds of color balance. This requires a level of skill and artistry that is not easy to come by. It also means that if a mistake is made, it must be used as is, reshot, or cut from the film. Digital editing allows the color of an image to be manipulated into thousands of possible choices at the touch of the button without any concern about losing the scene. The first film to employ digital coloring throughout, *O Brother, Where Art Thou?* (2000), wanted to give the footage an older washed-out image. This was accomplished easily and quickly with the new advancements in technology.

Special effects are almost central characters in some films today. Whether it be a *Transformer* film with more than 4000 special effects shots or *Life of Pi* (2012) in which more than 90% of the entire film is CGI (computer-generated image), the flexibility and sheer enormity of options digital editing offers makes it the choice of nearly all major motion pictures.

CAMERA

Earlier we discussed the drawbacks of the digital video cameras of the 1980s. It lacked depth of field and had a very limited dynamic range (the level of lightness and darkness it could record). The early video cameras were small hand-held devices that looked like anything a consumer could buy at a local electronics store for home video. It wasn't until the mid-1990s that enough advancements were made to create a true difference between consumer-level cameras and professional grade.

In 2005, the Panavision Genesis 35mm digital camera came out. It weighed 35 pounds and looked like a film camera. However, it lacked the ability to play back the scene on the camera itself. The Genesis also was still lacking the dynamic range that most directors and cinematographers desired. The industry changed almost overnight in 2007 with the introduction of the Red I camera. It had the clearest image to date, allowed for the greatest dynamic range available in a digital camera, and still had many of the desired abilities of a film camera. It did have two major drawbacks: It weighed 141 pounds and it crashed a lot. Often camera operators would tape ice packs to the camera to keep it from overheating. Although these drawbacks were not insignificant, the camera showed what was possible with digital cameras.

The most popular current models are the Red-Epic which now weighs less than 10 pounds and has 5200 pixels and the Apri-Alexa which has the dynamic range of a film camera. This has made it so that using a film camera seems almost ridiculous. As of today, all major camera manufacturers have stopped making film cameras. In 20 years a working film camera will be as rare as a working 8-track player.

Even the projectors in movie theaters are being replaced by digital versions. When *The Phantom Menace* came out in 1999, there were only four digital projectors in the United States; now the number is more than 4000. Not only is it quicker, cheaper, and easier to send movies around the country in digital format but it also means that every copy is as clear as the first reel off the negative; there is no degradation. It also means that there is no danger of it breaking or degrading from being shown. *Titanic* (1997) stayed in theaters so long that many of its film reels were disintegrating from being run through the projector so many times. With a digital version of the film that can never happen.

STORAGE

Does this mean the end of film entirely? Probably not. There is one area in which film outperforms digital and it's not even close: archiving. Photo chemical film is the only good archival source because it will never be format obsolete. You will always be able to access some sort of film projector. Since 1950, there have been 80 different formats of video, most of which can no longer be used. This is because the machines that they were made with no longer exist. For that reason alone it is unlikely that film will go away completely. The reason that we can go to YouTube and see *Arrival of a Train* nearly 120 years after it was made is because it was preserved on film.

SUMMARY

We find ourselves in the digital age of filmmaking. As technology improves digital will become more and more prevalent in the filmmaking process. The age of making movies with film cameras is ending soon and it is unlikely that anything will be able to save it. Digital editing has already virtually replaced the old style of film editing due to its speed, ease, and flexibility. Filming and projecting digitally is growing so quickly that it will soon drive photo chemical film out of that arena as well. Where film still stands strong is in its ability to store the images in such a way that we will always be able to have access to our film history.